GEOMETRIC HOOKED RUGS

Lizards and Ladders, 48" x 48", #3- to 5-cut wool on linen. Designed by Gail Dufresne and Norma Batastini. Hooked by Gail Dufresne, Lambertville, New Jersey, 2001.

GEOMETRIC HOOKED RUGS
Color & Design

GAIL DUFRESNE

Copyright© 2010 by Stackpole Books

Published by
STACKPOLE BOOKS
5067 Ritter Road
Mechanicsburg, PA 17055
www.stackpolebooks.com

2 9 1 0 0 3 7 4 1 2

On the front cover: *Starry Night*, designed and hooked by Gail Dufresne.
On the back cover: *Family Room Prototype*, designed and hooked by Gail Dufresne.
All photographs taken by Cindy Macmillan unless otherwise noted.

Library of Congress Cataloging-in-Publication Data

Dufresne, Gail.
Geometric Hooked Rugs: Color & Design /
Gail Dufresne.—1st ed..
    p. cm.

  ISBN 978-1-881982-71-5
  1. Rugs, Hooked—Patterns. I. Title.
  TT850.D84 2010
  746.7'4—dc22

CONTENTS

ACKNOWLEDGMENTS

I would like to thank my students who were so generous with their time, their rugs, and their enthusiasm for this project. I would like to thank Cindy Macmillan for taking the photographs. Thank you to my long-suffering husband who was always there to listen to me gripe, panic, and gloat throughout this process. I would especially like to acknowledge my mother, Doris LaPlante, and my sister, Yvonne Wood, without whom I never would have started on this journey that has completely changed my life and given me a purpose for living.

Thank you to all the wonderful students and friends who allowed me to share their work on these pages. I hope that these wonderful rugs will inspire others to design their own geometric hooked rugs and experience the excitement of the geometrics in their own works of art.

Allie Barchi	Jen O'Malley
Cathy Edwards	Cynthia Norwood
Carol Feeny	Sarah Province
Sue Green	Gail Schmidt
Kathleen Harwood	Corinne Watts
Barbara Kimbrough	Margaret Wenger
Doris LaPlante	Jana Whitelaw
Cindy Macmillan	Mary Jean Whitelaw
Patty Mahaffey	Yvonne Wood

Gail Dufresne has been hooking rugs since 1984. She began as a fine hooker because she loves detail, so she became a McGown certified teacher. More recently she has been working extensively with wide cuts and geometric designs. She is fascinated by color and finds that geometric designs allow her to indulge in her love of color and design.

Gail is always trying new techniques and going in new directions. She works with textures because she thinks that they give a rug depth that cannot be achieved with solid wool. She uses all types of unusual and non-traditional materials, such as ribbon, boucle, angora, chenille, glitter, and glitz. Gail's rugs have appeared in several issues of *Celebration of Hand-Hooked Rugs*, always showcasing her fresh and innovative look. She participated in the "Art of Playing Cards" project and served as a judge for Celebration XIX.

Dyeing is one of Gail's specialties. She teaches at camps and workshops throughout the United States, Canada, and England. Her rugs have appeared in many shows and exhibits over the past years. She has written several articles for *Rug Hooking* magazine, where she sits on the editorial board.

Gecko Inch Mat, 16" x 21", #8-cut wool on linen. Designed and hooked by Gail Durfesne, Lambertville, New Jersey, 2000.

CHAPTER ONE

What Is a Geometric and How It All Began

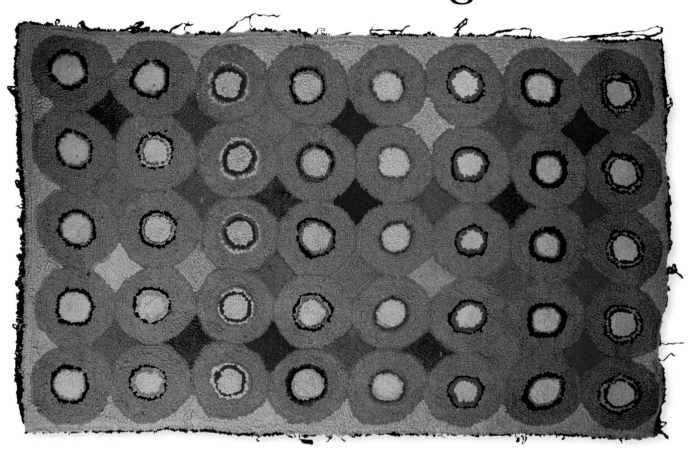

Simple lines are one of the most important elements of any design. Lines bring energy to our art: They are thick or thin, straight or curved. Lines give emphasis to ideas and they create patterns and a sense of direction. Creating a good design is all about managing the lines.

When we connect lines, we create shapes. The contrast of open, or negative, space around an enclosed shape gives the shape meaning, or defines it. Connected lines form geometric shapes—the squares, circles, rectangles, triangles, and polygons that we use in our designs.

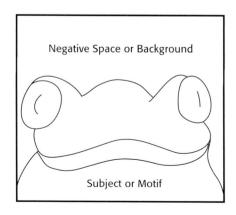

Negative Space or Background

Subject or Motif

Unnamed antique rug, 32" x 52", burlap. Designer, artist, and date completed unknown. From the collection of Cynthia Norwood.
By their nature, geometric rugs fit into any décor and color scheme.

Geometric shapes are everywhere—in our architecture, magazine layouts, furniture, and fabrics. Twentieth-century painters such as Picasso, Kandinsky, Frank Stella, M. C. Escher, and Vasarely revolutionized the art world when they showed that a full range of emotion can be expressed through simple, nonrepresentational geometric forms and colors, with no reference to nature. While more traditional artists represented the world in recognizable images, these artists explored the relationships between line, form, and color. Check out Victor Vasarely's bold, groundbreaking work. Widely considered the father of Op Art, his work is stunning and inspiring to artists everywhere.

From the beginning, hooked rugs have featured geometric shapes. The earliest examples of hooked rugs were the floor mats made in Yorkshire, England, during the early part of the 19th century. Rug hooking as we know it today started in the United States along the eastern seaboard and in Canada's Maritime Provinces.

In its earliest years it was a craft of poverty. The vogue for floor coverings in the United States came about after 1830 when factories began producing machine-made carpets for the rich. Poor women couldn't afford these carpets, so they continued to provide their own rugs, looking through their scrap bags for materials to use in creating their own homemade floor coverings. While girls from wealthy families were sent to school to learn embroi-

dery and quilting, rug hooking was never part of that curriculum, nor was it written about in popular ladies' magazines. It was considered a "country craft" in the days when the word "country," used in this context, was derogatory.

Since hooking was a craft of poverty, rug makers used whatever materials were available. Antique hooked rugs were created on burlap after 1850 because burlap was free—as long as there were old grain and feed bags available. Any scrap of fiber that was no longer usable as clothing was put to good use, often finding its way into a warm rug.

Geometric designs were used by some of the very first rug makers. Anyone with very basic skills could make a pleasing and utilitarian floor covering using a burlap sack, a handmade hook, some worn out clothing, and a bowl to trace around. As confidence and skill grew, a rug maker could learn to transform a two-dimensional design into a three-dimensional work of art by the effective use of color and perspective.

The majority of early hooked rugs were made by women, but men enjoyed the craft as well. Sailors made many fine rugs, preferring nautical or geometric themes over florals and scrolls. These first geometric rugs were workhorses, placed in front of sinks and fireplaces, and even used as covers for the woodpile when they were old and worn. Today hooked rugs are no longer considered merely practical. They are sought after because

Hearts and Star, 9" x 24", #8-cut wool on linen. Designed and hooked by Gail Dufresne, Lambertville, New Jersey, 2004.

Geometric rugs offer endless possibilities for designs. Simple shapes, as seen in this rug, are appealing and comfortable. Complicated geometric shapes are energetic and intriguing.

Opposite page: Unnamed antique rug, 18" x 32", wool strips on burlap. Designer, artist, and date completed unknown. From the collection of Cynthia Norwood.

Grid lines do not always have to be black. Often other colors can be used to add interest to a rug.

The simple, symmetrical layout of this antique rug is charming. Varied motifs, repeating throughout, move the viewer's eye around the rug. The dark grid lines guide your eye from top to bottom and side to side.

Gridded designs do not need to feature evenly spaced blocks. Random block sizes or repeating patterns can also be worked on a grid.

Grid lines do not have to be black. Think of them as another way to incorporate color into a rug. In this rug the light textured grid lines link the squares, lighten the color scheme, and allow the darker wools to shine.

they complement any decor, be it country, contemporary, or traditional.

Geometric rugs have always been popular, and they are still popular today among rug hookers. The designs can be simple or complex, muted in color or vibrant. There is no end to the variety, design, and colors in geometric rugs. That is what makes them so exciting to plan and satisfying to hook.

TYPES OF GEOMETRIC DESIGNS

The possibilities are endless when it comes to geometric hand-hooked rugs, especially if you consider designs that are comprised of both geometric and realistic, or organic, shapes. A simple circle design is easy to draw by tracing kitchen plates and glasses onto backing. A rug designed with heart shapes can be created by tracing boxes of chocolates. (The fun is to tell your sweetheart that you need as many different sizes of heart-shaped boxes of chocolates as he can find so that you can use them in your work!) You are limited only by your imagination.

Gridded Designs

A grid is a network of lines used to separate blocks or motifs. Every line in a composition is important in a design, with the potential to add interest. This premise is even true of geometric designs based on a grid. I have worked extensively with these types of gridded designs.

Most traditional Anglo-American quilt makers work with grids, using shapes pieced together within each block of the grid to form the overall design. The quilt maker then usually produces the overall larger pattern by repeating the design of one block in symmetrical and mirror-imaged versions in other blocks.

The grid lines themselves are important, though they are often discounted. Many people give little thought to color planning the lines. However, the grid lines should be treated as an integral part of the design because they are as important as any other design line. How an artist color plans these lines will directly influence the appearance of the motifs they separate.

Many people's first thought is that grid lines must be black. Not true! They do not have to be black, and in fact, they do not always have to be dark. Think of it this way: Grid lines simply give you another place to "hang" color. Consider using bright or colorful grid lines for a contemporary look.

Untitled, 17" x 26", #8-cut wool on linen. Designed and hooked by Gail Dufresne, Lambertville, New Jersey, 2001. I hooked a texture mat and saved small bits of the unhooked wool in photo protectors for reference.

Don't assume that grid lines have to be straight lines. The choice of whether to use straight, wavy, or even curved lines should be determined by the overall design and the artist's image of the rug.

Another myth about gridded designs is that the blocks separated by the grid lines must be the same size. Blocks *can* be identical in size, but they can also be various sizes placed at random throughout, or organized into a repeating pattern. The possibilities are endless indeed.

A gridded design can be as simple as Mary Jean Whitelaw's *Texture Mat,* which is a design comprised of 88 three-inch squares hooked with undyed textured wool from her stash. The end result is a very pleasing rug, and one she can refer to when she wants to see how a certain wool will look after it has been hooked. The grid lines and border of her rug were hooked with undyed textured wool.

Inch Mats

Inch mats are gridded designs traditionally associated with the rug makers of New England and Eastern Canada. A traditional inch mat design is a grid comprised of 1¼" squares—the extra ¼" allows for the grid lines—in which colors are arranged to form three adjacent diamonds with the central diamonds being larger than those on each side.

My *First Inch Mat,* page 10, measured 13" by 13" and was created as a small project for a local guild. I based its color plan on a design I found in *Great Patchwork: Working with Squares and Triangles,* a quilting book that contains page after page of color plans for gridded designs. It is a tremendous resource for inspiration, for quilters and rug hookers alike.

I find small inch mat designs to be the perfect canvas for experimenting with color and design. I make small samples that can be finished into pillows and footstools. These small projects allow me to experiment with new techniques. If I decide to abandon the piece because it isn't working, I do not have as much of a commitment— I've invested less time and fewer materials than I would have if I had tackled a larger piece. The inch squares can be worked individually, as in a mosaic tile pattern, or groups of squares can be worked together, leaving just corner and center motifs.

Opposite page: Mary Jean Whitelaw's *Texture Mat,* 26" x 38", #8-cut wool on linen. Designed and hooked by Mary Jean Whitelaw, Belle Mead, New Jersey, 1998. Pulling wool from your stash and hooking it in a gridded design makes an excellent reference for how a certain wool will hook up.

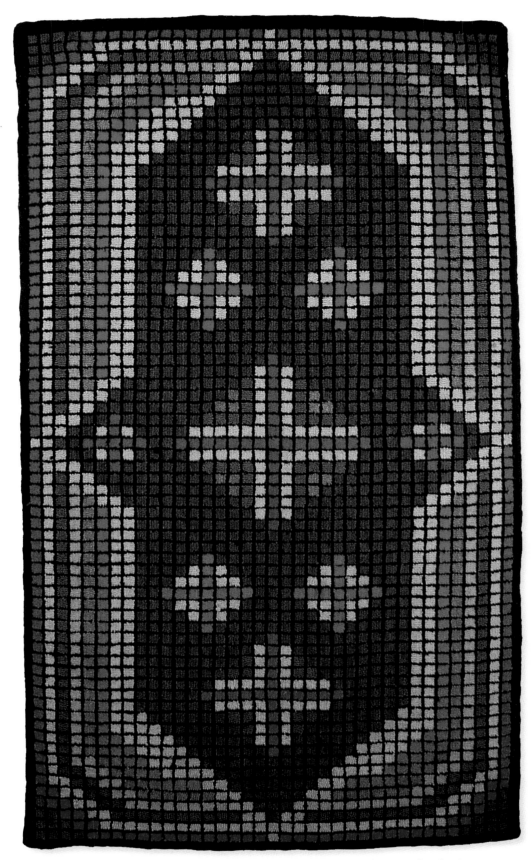

Traditional Yarn Inch Mat, 18" x 52", yarn on burlap. Designer, artist, and date completed unknown. From the collection of Gail Dufresne.

Traditional Inch Mat,
25" x 58", wool on burlap.
Designer, artist, and date
completed unknown. From
the collection of Gail Dufresne.

Mosaic tile patterns use
small squares and color to
create symmetrical geometric
shapes. Mosaic patterns were
as popular years ago as they
are today. Notice the brightly
colored sawtooth border,
which complements the
structured order of the tile
pattern.

First Inch Mat, 13" x 13", #3-cut wool on linen. Designed and hooked by Gail Dufresne, Lambertville, New Jersey, 1999.

My first inch mat was based on evenly spaced squares and a simple, dramatic color plan.

Froggy Inch Mat Footstool, 10" x 13", #3- and 5-cut wool, yarn, and leather on linen. Designed and hooked by Gail Dufresne, Lambertville, New Jersey, 2002.

Careful color planning allows the gridded design behind the frog take on a ripple effect.

Rose Inch Mat Footstool,
14" round, #3-cut wool on
linen. Designed and hooked
by Gail Dufresne, Lambertville,
New Jersey, 2000.

Every square that touched
any part of the rose or leaves
was hooked in solid black to
make the rose motif pop out
from the inch grid.

In addition to being great geometric designs on their own, inch mats provide a perfect background for superimposed images. I have a technique that I like to use for these designs. I often use just one color in all of the squares surrounding my superimposed motif, such as the black surrounding the rose in *Rose Inch Mat Footstool.* I hooked solid black in all of the squares touching any part of the rose or rose leaves and stem, to make them pop out from the grid. I then hooked the rest of the squares in a textured black wool that was more muted than the solid black. I hooked the grid lines in a red that was one value darker than the color used for the rose.

I took this idea of superimposing a realistic image over a grid one step further with *Froggy Inch Mat Footstool.* Each square that touched any part of the frog, his tongue, or the ladybug was hooked in

a black texture. Each square out from the black textured squares was hooked in a blue-purple. Finally, each square out from the purple squares was hooked in red-purple. I hooked the grid lines using a dip dye that incorporated many of the colors in the rest of the design, which gave the piece a pleasing balance.

Using an odd or even number of rows is crucial to the design of an inch mat. You must think this out in advance, considering your options. If, for instance, you want to alternate two colors, as I did in *Inch Mat Cat,* page 13, you will need an odd number of squares to end up with the same color in each corner of the design. The same principle is true for checkerboard borders. Of course, having different colors in the corners is not necessarily a bad thing depending on your design preferences! The corner squares in *Owl Inch*

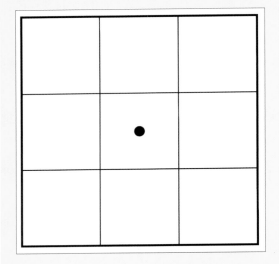

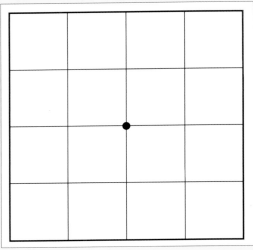

Find the center by folding the backing in half and then in half again. Mark the center with a dot. For an even number of squares, intersect the center dot with the grid line and work out from that center. For an odd number of squares, locate your first square around the center dot and work out from that square.

To draw a great-looking rug design, the grid lines on the backing must be straight, so be sure to choose a foundation with an even weave. Cotton rug warp works well for cuts less than a #7. Various thicknesses of linen are available to suit larger cuts. You can hook up to #8-cut wool in a 1" square. If you prefer, you can hook every other grid line, resulting in 2" squares.

1. Find the center of the backing by folding it in half, and then in half again. Open it and place a dot where the folds intersect. This dot marks the center.

2. If you want 1" squares in your rug, you'll need to draw 1¼" squares. The extra ¼" accommodates the grid lines.

3. Use a ruler to measure the first 1¼" square, then count the number of vertical threads within the square. If you want an odd number of grid lines, draw the first square so that it intersects the center line. If you want an even number of grid lines, start at the center line and measure out to the right of it and then to the left of it, working out toward the edge of the backing. Do not use a ruler to measure thereafter. Instead use a consistent thread count to determine the size of each square.

4. Using either a carpenter's pencil or a child's thick soft pencil, press down firmly between two vertical threads. (I love the My First Ticonderoga pencil, available at any office supply store.)

5. Make sure the pencil point remains in that groove as you move the pencil slowly down the backing. If the backing bunches up, ease the pressure on the pencil until the backing flattens. Do not lift the pencil off the surface. Repeat this procedure for the horizontal lines.

6. If you intend to superimpose a motif on top of the grid, first draw the gridded background over the entire design area with a pencil, and then draw the motif over the penciled grid.

7. Retrace the penciled grid lines with a permanent marker for a more visible pattern. If you superimposed a motif over the grid lines, do not retrace the sections of grid lines underneath the superimposed motif. The motif will stand out better from the penciled grid underneath it. I use

Detail of *Traditional Sunflower Inch Mat* showing the cross-over method of hooking grid lines.

Cross over the first grid line with the second instead of clipping at each intersection. In this photograph, the vertical line crosses over the horizontal line.

a Sharpie permanent industrial marker that remains permanent under most chemical washes and can withstand heat up to 500°F, or a Rub A Dub marker, which is expressly made for use on fabric. Do not use a regular Sharpie. The manufacturer states on the marker that regular Sharpies are "not for letter writing on cloth." Regular Sharpies—colored or black—can bleed onto wool and backing. I've seen it happen countless times.

How to Hook a Traditional Inch Mat Grid

Hook the grid lines first to hold the squares in place. Continue from the end of one short grid line section to the beginning of the next section by crossing over the intervening perpendicular or intersecting grid line. This way you will avoid cut ends at each intersection.

How to Hook the Squares to Fill in the Grid

Do not pack the loops inside the squares. Tightly packed loops will ruin the linear flow of the grid and push the backing out of shape.

Try hooking adjacent squares in alternate directions to reduce stress on the backing and add interest to the design. For example, hook the first square horizontally and the next square vertically. Another option to reduce stress on the backing is to hook each square in a circular motion, starting in the center and working out toward the border. Tip: To turn a corner without cutting a strip, turn the strip from underneath the backing so it is facing the direction in which you wish to hook, then proceed.

Owl Inch Mat, 15" x 18", #3- to 8-cut wool on linen. Designed and hooked by Gail Dufresne, Lambertville, New Jersey, 2002.

An even number of squares in each row and column will put different color squares in each corner.

Mat are different colors, but you have to look twice to even notice it.

Drawing out a color plan on paper before diving in to the hooking process may save you time. Try constructing a grid on paper and coloring it with crayons or colored pencils. Time spent carefully planning often eliminates surprises later on.

Inch Mat Cat, 12" x 16", #3- to 8-cut wool on linen. Designed and hooked by Gail Dufresne, Lambertville, New Jersey, 2002.

If you're using two alternating background colors, place an odd number of squares in each row and column to end up with the same color in each corner.

Spools, 28" x 46", #8-cut wool on monk's cloth. Designed and hooked by Gail Dufresne, Lambertville, New Jersey, 1996. Careful planning of colors and values change the look of a basic log cabin pattern into something totally unexpected. The log cabin design disappears and colorful spools emerge.

Log Cabin, 26" x 38", #8-cut wool on linen. Designed and hooked by Sue Green, Easton, Maryland, 2005.
    Creating an optical illusion within a log cabin design requires careful preplanning that usually involves colored pencils and paper.

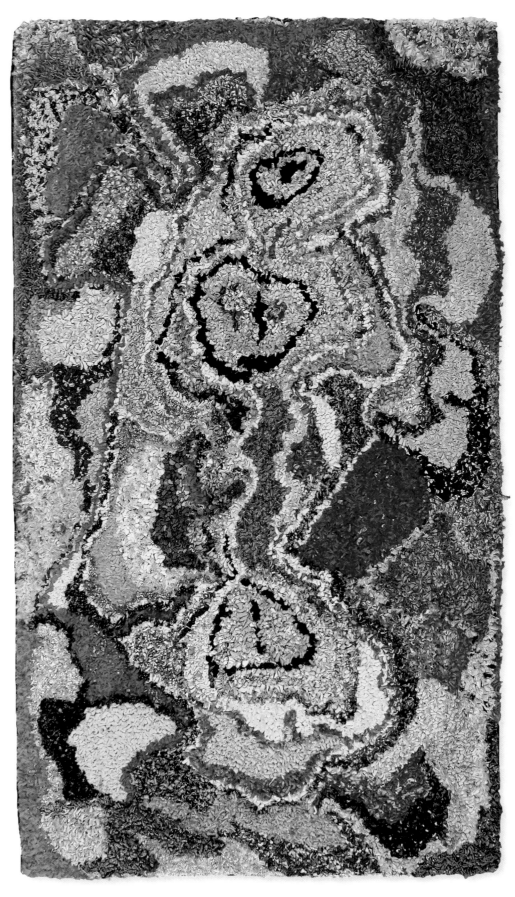

Antique Abstract, 22" x 38". Designer, artist, materials, and date completed unknown. From the collection of Barbara Kimbrough.

Abstract rugs are considered to be part of the geometric family of rugs. This traditional abstract features no recognizable shapes, just puddles of color and swirling lines.

Integrated Boxers, 27" x 39", #8-cut wool and mixed media on linen. Designed and hooked by Mary Jean Whitelaw, Belle Mead, New Jersey, 2010.

Tessellation and a gridded design are combined to create a geometric rug full of motion and whimsey.

Log Cabin Designs

Another very common gridded design which is also a quilt design is called the log cabin. These designs can be treated as simple repeating patterns, or by effective placement of value and chroma, you can make an unlimited number of stunning three-dimensional designs.

If you are planning to create an optical illusion with a log cabin design, knowing the number of blocks you need is crucial. Note for instance Sue Green's *Log Cabin,* page 15. In order to create the illusion that Sue wanted, she needed four blocks across her design and six blocks down.

Abstract Designs

Not all geometric designs are gridded. Unlike traditional Anglo-American quilt makers, African-American strip quilt makers worked with virtually no templates or tools, not even rulers, cutting shapes from scraps by eye, creating visually stunning designs that were not symmetrical or grid-

ded. For an excellent book on African American strip quilting, refer to *The Quilts of Gee's Bend.*

Abstract art explores the relationships between line, form, and color with no obvious reference to recognizable images. Barbara Kimbrough's *Antique Abstract* is an excellent example, with no organic shapes, grid lines, or symmetrical blocks, just wonderful swirling lines and puddles of all sorts of mixed media materials in colors that coax the eye to travel all around the rug.

For a more detailed discussion of abstraction and abstract designs, see chapter six.

Tesselations

A tessellation is a design where a shape or tile repeats to fill a space without any gaps or overlaps. In its simplest form, bathroom floor tiles or brick paths or inch mats are tessellations. The types of designs that most people associate with

Jana's Celtic, 16" round, #4-cut wool on linen. Designed and hooked by Jana Whitelaw, Princeton, New Jersey, 2010.

Celtic designs can be reworked to create intricate geometric rugs.

tessellations are the interlocking patterns of the type for which artist M. C. Escher is famous.

Mary Jean Whitelaw's mat of her favorite subject, boxer dogs, is a clever example of a tessellation. The boxers fit together like jigsaw puzzle pieces. The entire design, when initially drawn, was of interlocking boxers, but rather than hooking them all, Mary Jean hooked blocks of color in some of the areas. The center tessellated section is the playful focus of the rug.

Celtic Designs

Celtic designs are a different kind of geometric design. These complex, puzzling designs are characterized by interwoven ropes of intricate knot work. The trick to color planning these rugs is to follow the unbroken lines that weave through the entire design like a maze. A great reference book to learn more

about these designs is *Celtic Spirals and Other Designs,* by Sheila Sturrock.

ORIENTALS

Oriental designs are an interesting subset of geometric designs. Some are comprised of all geometric shapes, and some combine both geometric and organic shapes. For an excellent reference book on the history of Oriental carpets refer to *Oriental Carpets: Their Iconology and Iconography From Earliest Times to the 18th Century.* Take a close look at an Oriental and you will see the intricate nature and color planning that go into the planning and execution of these complex designs.

COPYRIGHT ISSUES

Simple geometric shapes such as hearts and stars in and of themselves cannot be copyrighted, but you cannot assume that any geometric design found on a

Kazak-istan, 26" x 44", #5-cut wool on linen. Designed by Pearl McGown. Hooked by Gail Dufresne, Lambertville, New Jersey, 2000.

Mae Ling, 35" x 58", #3-cut wool on linen. Designed by Fraser. Hooked by Margaret Wenger, Lancaster, Pennsylvania, 2010.

Oriental #33, 31" x 55", #4-cut on burlap. Designed by Fraser Patterns. Hooked by Doris LaPlante, East Hartford, Connecticut, 1983. IMPACT XPOZURES

Diamond in the Square,
55" x 55", #3-, 5-, 6-, and 8-
cut wool on linen. Designed
and hooked by Kathleen
Harwood, Montrose,
Pennsylvania, 2009.
Kathleen's inspiration was a
traditional Amish quilt
pattern, full of geometric
shapes. Her comtemporary
interpretation of this
traditional design shows the
possibilities when we look at
geometric designs with
imagination. KATHLEEN HARWOOD

greeting card or magazine cover is not subject to copyright law. Common basic geometric shapes can be subject to copyright protection if they are part of a selection and arrangement that rises to the level of creativity required under the law. If the original designer has registered any design copyrights and if they are infringed upon, he or she can seek substantial monetary damages, including the defendant's profits, any of the designer's lost profits, and his or her attorneys' fees and costs for bringing the lawsuit. Many quilting designs and design elements (such as the log cabin design and checkerboard borders of black and white squares) are in the public domain and therefore available for use by anyone.

If you are in doubt about what you can or cannot use, check the website of the United States Copyright office (*www.copyright.gov*), an excellent source for definitive information regarding copyright law.

I once felt I needed to ask permission to use a geometric design when I adapted an assembly diagram featured in a quilting book called *Easy Does It Quilts*. I contacted the publisher and was told that I did not need permission to copy the diagram. But I thought that it was such a distinctive design that I would never have developed it on my own. I have exhibited this rug but never sold it. I do not feel that it is my design to sell.

CHAPTER TWO

Color Gets the Credit
But Value Does the Work
The Value of Value, Contrast, and Intensity

Froggy, 8" x 8", #3- to #8-cut wool on linen. Designed and hooked by Gail Dufresne, Lambertville, New Jersey, 2000.

Once you've found or designed a geometric pattern you'd like to hook, the next step is to work on a color plan. A color plan can be as elaborate and time consuming as coloring in a full-size pattern with colored pencils or as quick and simple as laying strips of wool side-by-side.

By working with geometric designs, I discovered that the key to any effective color plan is to understand the concept of value. Color is important—but value is critical. Learning "the value of value" is probably the most important aspect of color planning. Value is a major design element, and once you understand how designs

23

Pinwheel Puddles, 38"x 28", #6-cut wool on linen. Designed and hooked Jen O'Malley, Telford, Pennsylvania, 2010.

Ruby Pearl, 16" x 16", #3- to 8-cut wool and mixed fibers on linen. Designed and hooked by Gail Dufresne, Lambertville, New Jersey, 2002.

The placement of the bright yellow in the middle square in front of Ruby Pearl was not an accident. In effect, I hooked an arrow pointing right to Ruby's face so that it is clear that he is the star of the show.

Ruby Pearl is clearly visible in front of the background squares. If he faded into the background it would be because the values used in the goat and the squares were too close.

are created by the effective use of value, you will be one step closer to understanding how to work with color effectively.

UNDERSTANDING VALUE, CONTRAST, AND INTENSITY

Value refers to the relative lightness or darkness of a color. Whether a color is perceived as light or dark depends on the value of the color next to it. A pink strip of wool next to a red strip of red wool is perceived as light. The same pink strip of wool next to a white strip of wool is perceived as dark.

One of my most influential teachers, Marjorie Judson, said in every class: "No color stands alone." I adapt her statement a bit and say, "No value stands alone." Everything is relative when you start working with color and value. Color may

enhance a design but value establishes and solidifies the design. So instead of starting with a color plan, the way we were all taught, start by thinking in terms of a value plan.

Contrast between light and dark is what makes a design visible to the viewer. The whole impact of the design can be lost if you don't consider the values of its parts. If you hook a motif in the same value as the space around it, you will not be able to see the motif.

Intensity is equally important. Intensity, sometimes called "chroma," refers to the relative brightness of a color. In its purest, most brilliant state, an intense color is completely saturated and has not been diluted by any other color. A color is diluted, becoming more and more neutral, when white, black, gray, or any other color

Goat Hill, 31" x 52", #3- to 8-cut wool on linen. Designed and hooked by Gail Dufresne, Lambertville, New Jersey, 2002.
A little bit of bright color goes a long way. While the background appears to be all brights, a closer look reveals the darks and dulls.

is added. If you add white to the color red, it becomes pink. Adding black or gray to red lessens its intensity, creating a duller red. Adding another color, such as blue, will make it more purple, less saturated, and therefore a less intense red.

Intensity works just like value when planning a rug. It does not matter what color you use to give your rug a bit of pizzazz, but that color must be a little brighter, or more intense, than the rest of the wool. Hooked sparingly, this accent color, sometimes called "poison," stands out among the other colors and will add interest. It is best to vary the amounts of accent color rather than placing equal amounts all through the piece. Variety surprises the eye.

In *Ruby Pearl,* I hooked the goat atop vibrant squares that were filled with a relatively medium value #8-cut wool—except for just one strip of a brighter #3-cut wool hooked into each square. The brightest colors are hot pink, lime green, and yellow. Some squares have a longer strip of bright wool than others. The point is that the chroma of each little piece of these bright colors is similar in each square.

At first glance, the background of *Goat Hill* appears to be all bright colors. I did, indeed, use several bright colors—orange, bright pink, and an especially loud chartreuse. But look again and you will see dull colors as well, such as dull purple, maroon, and dark green. A little brightness goes a long way.

Ace of Hearts, 16" x 26", #3- to 8-cut wool and yarn on linen. Designed and hooked by Gail Dufresne, Lambertville, New Jersey, 2003. The center heart pops right out of very bright colors because it was hooked in black and white—the highest possible contrast.

Light wool

Black wool

Dark wool

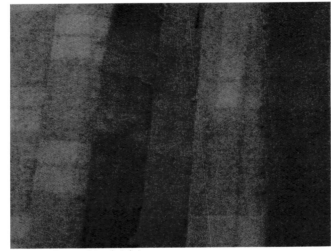

Red Pendleton shirt (bright)

USING ALL THREE

Now that you understand how value, contrast, and intensity work individually, it's time to make them work together in your rug. Here's the basic concept.

1. A greater difference in value creates a greater contrast.

2. The greatest contrast in value and the most intense color should be placed at the center of interest, the focal point.

For the greatest impact, put very dark next to very light, and very bright next to very dull. Then use that approach in the motif you most want to accentuate, the focal point of the rug. Of course, the highest contrast possible is black beside white. In *Ace of Hearts*, the viewer's eye is brought right to the center of the rug, to the black and white squares in the heart. This is the part of the playing card that I wanted to stand out most.

Geometric designs are perfect for learning this concept. Squares, circles, and triangles can be any color. Obviously, there is no correct color for a rectangle. Because there are no realistic objects with which to associate color, you can focus on the impact that value, contrast, and intensity have on your design.

The Way I Learned the Lesson

This is how I learned the value of value, and the meaning and importance of intensity. One of my first students wanted help hooking a log cabin. She showed me a photo of a black and white log cabin rug. I decided to hook one. What I did not realize until sometime later was that the method I used to color plan the design proved to be an invaluable lesson in the importance of considering the

Wools for the log cabin designs fall into four categories in terms of intensity and value.

First Log Cabin, 26" x 38", #8-cut wool on linen. Designed and hooked by Gail Dufresne, Lambertville, New Jersey, 2000.

I like the diversity of using different cuts and do not find much difference in a wool strip that was cut ¹/₃₂" narrower or wider than another strip.

Tip: When mixing cuts, bring the narrower-cut wool higher than you normally would, to the height of the wider-cut strips.

value of a color, rather than relying simply on the color.

I had never seen a log cabin quilt design before, so my mind was geared toward using the values I saw in the black and white photo to plan the rug, not toward any particular colors. I could tell from the photo that I needed areas of relative darkness and lightness, and I began to organize my wool according to value.

I made rules for myself: The wool had to be "as is," nothing that was overdyed. It couldn't be solid. I wanted only textures, like tweeds and plaids. It had to be recycled wool or wool from previous projects—no "good wool" (meaning I couldn't use yardage that was neatly folded or on bolts, waiting for a new project).

I picked two items to be the constants in the rug: the grid lines and the chimneys (the squares in the middle of the block). For the grid lines, I chose a black wool. For the chimneys, I found the perfect red in a Pendleton shirt, which was a little brighter than the other wools I selected. That was the only solid material I used.

I made two piles of wool for the log cabins: one dark and one light. In terms of value and intensity, I was working with a light, a medium, a dark (black) and a bright (red), illustrated on page 28.

Another rule I made was that I could not pick which wool went where, meaning that I had to dive into the value bags and use the piece that I grabbed. No careful choosing allowed. All the different reds, blues, greens, and so on were hooked just as they came out of the bag.

I made adjustments as I hooked, transferring a light texture to the dark bag when necessary, or vice versa. I found that some medium values worked on both the dark and the light side, and I liked the continuity that this gave me. I did not know it at the time, but I was making relative value adjustments. Every single piece of wool worked beautifully except for a gold and black buffalo plaid. The gold was just too bright to fit in on either side, even in small doses. It threw off the balance of the design.

Log Cabin Spin, 48 ¹/₂" x 69 ¹/₂", #8-cut wool on linen. Design adapted from Georgia Bonesteel's *Log Cabin Spin,* published in *Easy-Does-It-Quilts* (Oxmoor House, 1995). Hooked by Gail Dufresne, Lambertville, New Jersey, 2001.

Assembly diagram for Georgia Bonesteel's *Log Cabin Spin* quilt, published in *Easy-Does-It-Quilts* (Oxmoor House, 1995). Reprinted with permission.

If I hooked in a piece of wool that really seemed to scream out at me, I waited a day or so, continued to hook, and then I looked again. I was not quick to remove any wool that seemed to stand out as a little brighter than the rest. Sometimes that bright spark worked out.

I used #8-cut wool, unless I found narrower cut leftovers that fit all of my rules. I loved the idea of using all leftover materials. This style seemed to be in keeping with the tradition of those first rug makers who used whatever they had on hand. The final rug was a success, and I learned an amazing amount about values and how they interact.

Adding Another Value

As soon as I was finished, I started to search for another design to continue my journey into the world of value planning. I needed a project that would teach me how contrast is achieved when differing values are adjacent to each other.

I found it in a quilt called *Log Cabin Spin* wall hanging, a design featured in renowned quilter Georgia Bonesteel's book, *Easy Does It Quilts*. The book included an assembly diagram, and I immediately saw how it could take my value plan lesson one step further. If you look at the border you can see that there is an additional value. So in addition to light, medium, dark, and bright, this project included a medium dark value as well.

I used the same wool from my *First Log Cabin*, but I took all of the relatively bright red textures out of the medium dark bag and put them into the bright bag along with my red Pendleton shirt. I also took all of the darkest textures from the medium dark bag and mixed those with solid black skirts. I worked out of these five bags instead of four: light, medium, medium dark, dark, and bright. I worked in the same manner as I did with the first rug, randomly pulling wool from the five bags.

Light wool

Medium wool

Medium dark wool

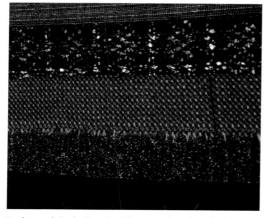

Dark wool, including braiding wool and multicolored polyester fabric

Bright red wool, with red plaids

The hardest part of this rug was getting the very dark "black" circle to stand out from the medium dark area. I ended up using one of my braiding wools and a black textured, shiny material that I suspect is polyester.

This proved to be a tricky rug to hook. I had to pay strict attention to the diagram because it was easy to mix up the values. Even though I checked the rug constantly for errors, I did not find my final mistake until I took a photograph of the finished rug. Something didn't look right: I had reversed a light and a dark area.

Log Cabin Spin Too, 48 ¹/₂" x 69 ¹/₂", yarn and #3- to ¹/₂"-cut wool on linen. Adapted from Georgia Bonesteel's *Log Cabin Spin* and hooked by Gail Dufresne, Lambertville, New Jersey, 2001.

As a variation on *Log Cabin Spin*, I made the design more my own by superimposing several motifs that I had hooked in the past: a goat, a sheep, sunflowers, lizards, and frogs.

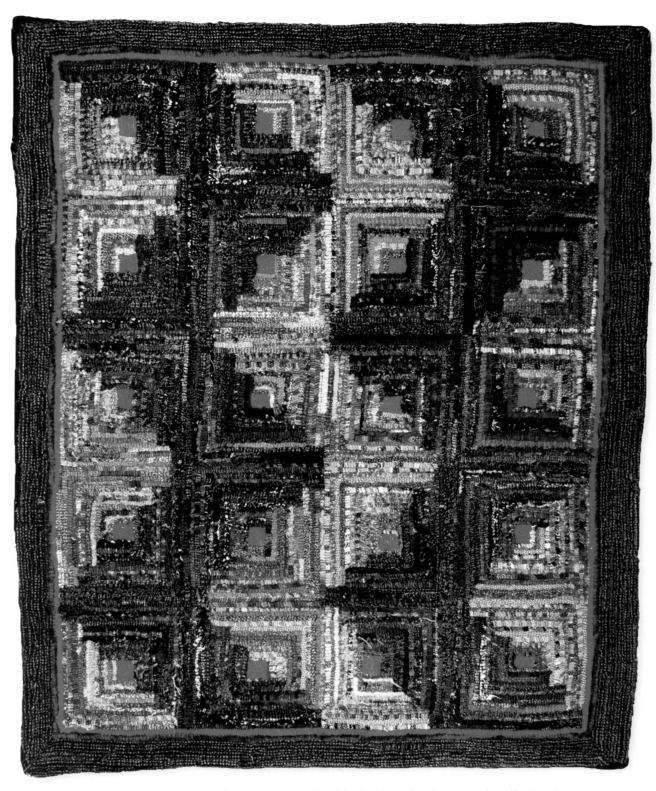

Zig Zag Log Cabin, 32" x 39", #8-cut wool on linen. Designed and hooked by Gail Dufresne, Lambertville, New Jersey, 2002. This study in low contrast uses fewer lighter and brighter values than the previous log cabin designs.

Wool for Zig Zag Log Cabin:

Medium wool

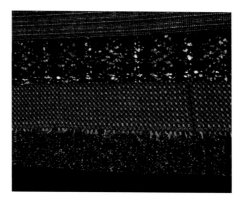

Dark wool, including braiding wool and multicolored polyester fabric

Red wool

Working with Low Contrast

Since I loved the low contrast in the medium and medium dark border of *Log Cabin Spin*, I decided to try my hand at a low-contrast rug. My *Zig Zag Log Cabin*, left, needed wool that was close in value, so I removed some of the lighter, brighter values in order to achieve the lower contrast. I added many beautiful grayed reds, which were much lower in intensity than the center reds and did not detract from their spark in the chimneys.

I used to think that what made a design interesting and unique was its color plan, and that is what most of us think. But hooking these three rugs helped me understand that value can simplify the color planning process. It sounds confusing at first, but careful thought and observation will help you understand this important point. Considering materials strictly as light or dark, or dull or bright, eliminates a lot of confusion. When the element of color is added back into the planning after values have been determined, it is much easier to make color decisions.

Once you grasp this concept, you will no longer have to reinvent the wheel each time you begin a new project. You will be one step closer to understanding how to work with color effectively. Value is the key.

The Value of Value

Before I learned the value of values, each rug was a new struggle. When I ran into a problem, I instinctively thought in terms of color instead of value. The error of my ways became crystal clear as I was working out the color plan for *Lizards and Ladders*.

I was working on this rug at a workshop, and I was trying to decide what colors to use in the 3" squares of the game board portion of the rug. I tried many equally light values of different colors: peach, lemon, aqua, ecru, and so on. I hooked two colors, then more, into many of the 3" squares. Then I stood back and tried to figure out which color worked best. I couldn't decide, so I asked my teacher and everyone else who walked past. Each person chose a different color—what was going on?

As it turned out, I had intuitively chosen the correct *value*, so the *color* was irrelevant. I didn't take out any of the colors, and then people thought I was a genius because I had used all the colors in my little squares. Since learning the value of values, I know that almost any "color

Closeup of *Lizards and Ladders*. (See the full rug on page ii.)

Starry Night, 45" x 45", #8-cut wool on linen. Designed and hooked by Gail Dufresne, Lambertville, New Jersey, 2002. Only two colors were used in this rug, but each color has many different values.

problem" is really a problem of value or intensity.

I planned the blue and yellow *Starry Night* after I fully understood and had intellectualized the value of values. I called on my knowledge of values, and chose just two colors, blue and yellow—but I used several values of each. I had learned that an effective color plan is possible using just a few colors if these colors include several different values and levels of intensities. I used all undyed, as-is wool, both solid and textured. From the center to the border of the rug, the values run from light to dark and the intensity runs from bright to dull.

Once you grasp the concept that it is not the color but the value that matters, you can start to mix all sorts of wool together for a much more interesting look. You can also stop worrying about running out of wool. I have had students who would rather not use their first choice of wool because they were paralyzed with fear that they would run out and not be able to find an exact match. Using one color over and over again is nowhere near as interesting as using several colors that vary a bit but are close enough in value that they "read" the same. Everything you hook can be done in wools that are sorted by value and intensity, not by color. Just think: You can sort the leftovers from all of your other projects into relative value piles that can be used over and over for future projects! Organization has never been easier.

EVALUATING YOUR WORK

If you're like most of the rug hookers I know—myself included—you work right on top of your rug, with your eyes only inches from your work. Unfortunately, what looks clearly defined at that close angle and proximity may appear as a sea of middle values when you look at the rug from a distance. Make a point to periodically step away from your work to really evaluate it. The long view will tell you if the values are working the way you intended.

I hook in my family room every night, and I don't allow myself to watch any television— not even the news or weather—unless I am hooking. When I am done hooking for the evening, I take the piece out of my hoop and place it over the top of my chair. I look at it before I go to bed, and even if I think it looks abysmal, I never change anything that night because I know I am too tired and too close to the work. I leave the piece on the back of the chair, turn the light on in the morning before my chores, and look at it from several angles as I walk in and out and around the room. If I am really stumped, or if I don't think it is working right, I move it to the sofa and work on another piece while I evaluate where I went wrong. If I still can't figure out what I am not satisfied with, I resort to one of the following techniques.

Tools to Help Determine Value

Photocopying. When I am stuck, this is the method I turn to most often. A black and white image from a photocopier removes color as a factor and gives me a better idea of how the values interact. I actually photocopy the area in the rug which is giving me trouble. Photocopying usually reveals two common errors:

1) The piece lacks depth because no dark values were used.

2) The motif fades into the background because the contrast between the negative space around the motif and the motif itself is not strong enough.

Transparent red plastic. Place strips of wool under red plastic and take a good look. The image is not as strong as a black and white image, but the red plastic eliminates the colors so you can see the value of each wool in relation to the others. Look for other simple color and value tools that will help you choose correctly.

Reducing glass, binoculars, or a door peephole. Each of these will put the illusion of distance between you and your work so you can view your work from farther away without physically moving. Often when you are close to your work, the contrast seems sufficient and the design appears to be working well. However, when you move away from your work, you may find that two values blend together and that the contrast is lost. You can purchase a peephole cheaply at any hardware store.

Camera. Looking through a camera lens is similar to looking at an object through a reducing glass because the camera lens makes

Vulture Inch Mat,
16" x 18", #3- to 6-
cut wool on linen.
Designed by
Gail Dufresne and
Norma Batastini.
Hooked by
Gail Dufresne,
Lambertville,
New Jersey, 2000.
The dark feathers
contrast nicely with
the bright, colorful
background
squares.

the image smaller. When you look through a camera lens, one eye is closed and the open eye sees only what is in the view of the lens. Your peripheral vision is cut off so your eye can concentrate only on what is in front of it. Another helpful technique is to take photos of your work as you make changes. Color photos work, but black and white pictures will eliminate the colors and put your focus on values. One photo in color and one in black and white is ideal.

Mirror. Use a mirror to evaluate your work from a new angle. Everything is reversed as you look at your rug in a mirror, so your perspective is different, providing you with a new view. You may be surprised at what you see when you look at a reversed image.

A VALUE-ADDED EXERCISE

If you're still a little shaky on the concept of value, try this experiment. Pull out some of your wool, and throw it on the table or floor. Sort it into five piles from the lightest value to the darkest. It can get tricky! Sort the wool into these values:

1. Light values
2. Medium light values
3. Medium values
4. Medium dark values
5. Dark values

When you're finished, you'll have a well-sorted wool stash with a wide selection of relative light, medium, and dark wool.

The true value of this exercise is that you'll discover what values of wool you are missing. You may lack light- or dark-valued wools—or both—and have lots and lots of pretty medium-valued wools. Or you may have light and dark wools with very little of those medium values in between. In either case, the missing values will make it hard for you to transition from one value to the next, putting you at a disadvantage when it comes to efficient value planning. Remember: you need subtle value changes in your wool to transition from one value to another without a great skip in the process.

The ultimate stash is one that has all of the colors of the color wheel in all values.

CHAPTER THREE

Color: You Know More Than You Think You Know!

Family Room Prototype #3, 22" x 34", #6-cut wool and yarn on linen. Designed and hooked by Gail Dufresne, Lambertville, New Jersey, 2008.

Color is personal. We all see and use color in our own unique way. What designs appeal to us, the way we put colors together, the textures we choose—these are reflections of our individuality. There are no rights or wrongs. It is important to have the courage to follow your own instincts, even if your preferences vary greatly from those of everyone around you.

Jinny Beyer tells a funny and enlightening story in her book *Color Confidence for Quilters.* When she was in third grade, Jinny adored coloring with her favorite color combination of purple and pink. One day her teacher grabbed the two crayons out of her hand and cackled loud enough for the whole class to hear, "Pink and purple don't go together! I don't ever want to see you using pink and purple together again!" She then

Family Room Prototype #2, 21" x 21", #6-cut wool plus yarns on linen. Designed and hooked by Gail Dufresne, Lambertville, New Jersey, 2008.

marched Jinny up to the front of the classroom, snapped the crayons in half, and threw them in the trash. Not very encouraging to a budding artist!

To this day I am told that the colors I choose are childlike and garish. A few have even assured me not to worry, that my palette will mature. As an adult, I have learned to ignore the uninvited remarks of critics. I just try to keep moving forward on my chosen color path.

Moving forward is not always easy, though. Remember when people were rushing to have their colors analyzed and then would never buy any article of clothing that did not exactly match the swatches the colorist gave them? We are so insecure about our own color decisions that we are willing to let a total stranger tell us what colors we should wear!

Family Room Prototype #1, 8" x 31", #6-cut wool plus yarns on linen. Designed and hooked by Gail Dufresne, Lambertville, New Jersey, 2008.

I remember my defining moment, the moment I started to trust my own color sense. I was in a design class with Marjorie Judson, one of my favorite teachers, at the Green Mountain Rug School in Randolph Center, Vermont. I designed a very simple spool rug, but for me it was a major turning point because it was the first complete rug that I had designed on my own. I started working in the wool I had chosen. Marjorie soon told me that my colors were too bright, but I opted to continue in the intensity that I preferred. On the last day of the class, each student shared her work with the rest of the class. Marjorie prefaced each of our rug unveilings with some encouraging words. When it was my turn, she announced that she had thought my colors were too bright, but that I kept at it and I made them work. To this day that incident remains one of the biggest turning points in my rug hooking career: To thine own self be true.

DEVELOP YOUR OWN COLOR SENSE

To begin developing your own color sense, learn as much as you can about your personal preferences. Be willing to open your eyes to new ideas and insights. Find colors that reflect your personality and style, even if they differ radically from those of your friends. And if any teacher tells you that the colors you use are wrong, find a new teacher!

If you really want to explore your true color preferences but have always felt obligated to choose colors that match the decor in your house, take a color break. Play with color just for the sheer joy of it. I think along the lines of a T-shirt I have: "Real art won't match your sofa." I have rarely, if ever, felt that I had to use colors that will match any room in my house. Rug hooking is how I express myself artistically, so that frees me from the burden of feeling that my rugs must have some utilitarian value or fit into some decorating scheme.

Kentucky Montage, 20" x 27", #3- and #4- cut wool on rug warp. Designed by Melissa Elliott. Hooked by Sarah Province, Silver Spring, Maryland, 2009.

Gecko Inch Mat, 16" x 21", #8-cut wool on linen. Designed and hooked by Gail Dufresne, Lambertville, New Jersey, 2000. A stuffed toy gecko, below, was the inspiration for this inch mat design.

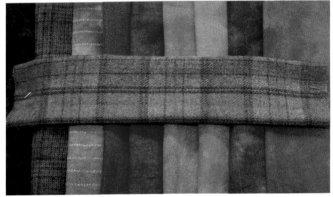

This photo shows one of Rebecca Erb's plaid wools, called Marie's Magnificent Mix, with wool pulled from the colors in the plaid. The color that might be overlooked is the taupey neutral that by itself is not terribly pretty or interesting, but it acts as a beautiful transition for the other material.

Don't be afraid to experiment and make mistakes. When I start a new rug, I usually hate the way it looks. I force myself to keep going. I keep changing colors or values or intensity until I eventually see order emerge from the chaos and I like

Closeup of *Geometric Pot Pourri.* (See the full rug on page 73.)

the results. I do a lot of pulling out along the way—that is all part of the process.

When experimenting with new techniques or different color schemes, don't start with a huge design. I usually choose a small piece—a foot stool, a tabletop piece, or a wall hanging—as a prototype so I can work out the glitches before I tackle a larger piece of work. Because they are small, I usually finish them, and some have become my favorite pieces. The rug on page 39, for example, is one of the prototypes for a full-sized family room rug. I never got to the room-sized rug, but I have two beautiful tabletop-sized pieces with the design concept worked out, and a third piece that hangs on my family room wall. If I ever get to the floor rug, I will have finished examples already worked out and will not have to start from the very beginning—unless I decide to move in a whole new direction!

Free yourself from the stagnation caused by feeling that you can't start something new until you have finished all the projects that you have started. It is okay to abandon a piece that isn't working. You only have so much time to create, so why spend that time working on something you don't like?

Take the Time to Observe

I believe the most useful skill for an artist is observation. Slow down and look at the world around you. See the relationship between objects, colors, and shapes. Learning to see is the key to inspiration.

Learning to see helps you understand color. Color inspiration is all around you—in photographs, fabrics, paint chips, wallpaper, advertisements, magazines, and garden layouts. It leaps out at you when you least expect it.

Keep a notebook, journal, or sketchbook to hold your photos, sketches, fabric

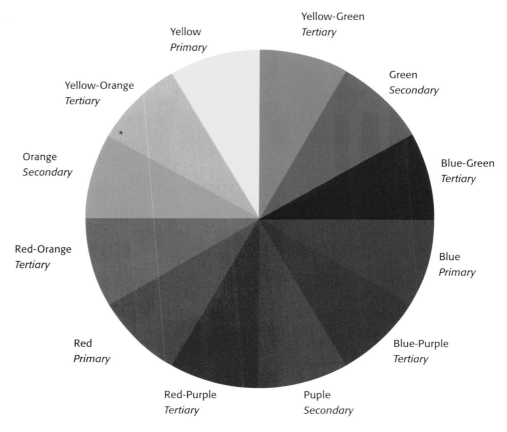

Yellow
Primary

Yellow-Green
Tertiary

Green
Secondary

Blue-Green
Tertiary

Blue
Primary

Blue-Purple
Tertiary

Puple
Secondary

Red-Purple
Tertiary

Red
Primary

Red-Orange
Tertiary

Orange
Secondary

Yellow-Orange
Tertiary

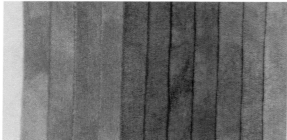

Wool dyed to show twelve steps along the color wheel.
Classic color schemes will help you design appealing and
lively rugs. IMPACT XPOZURES

samples, and ideas. These gathered inspirations
become your visual aids. When you are ready to
design or color plan a new piece, select a favorite
from your collection to use as inspiration. When
something first catches your eye, you may not know
how it will work into a future vision, but if you notice
it, it is important. Keep an open mind, and let your
ideas gradually evolve.

As an example, take a look at how my *Gecko Inch
Mat*, page 42, developed. While on a weekend trip to
Vermont, an intricate grid pattern from Flinders
Petrie's *Decorative Symbols and Motifs for Artist's and
Craftspeople* intrigued me. I drew it on some backing
and decided to figure out a color plan. Later that
weekend, I bought a stuffed gecko covered in a wild

fabric comprised of multicolored squares. When I got back to the motel, I tossed the gecko down, and it landed on top of the grid. That simple act inspired me to super-impose the gecko over the inch mat. So I traced it, and used the gecko's fabric as my color plan.

One of the best places to look for a color combination that suits you is in your wool stash. What colors are in your stash? What is your favorite wool? Why do you love it? Take a look at the wool and analyze every color you see. Be sure not to discount the neutrals or any odd colors that you think are not interesting. Unfortunately, we usually prefer those pretty middle values and forget the dark and light values that are necessary to make the design work. This tendency is a major roadblock in our design process. Those neutral values and odd colors are the ones that make the others sing. Without them we are left with a muddled sea of middle values.

DEMYSTIFYING THE COLOR WHEEL

The aura and mystery of the color wheel looms over us like a heavy shadow. We often feel we need to totally understand color theory in order to be able to work with the wheel comfortably. We hesitate to make simple color

decisions. As a result we are constrained by what we think the color wheel dictates rather than taking risks, experimenting, and trying different combinations. The great news for those of us without any formal art training is that we don't need to be a color expert to learn to use color effectively.

In my experience, working intuitively with color is more successful in helping us learn about color than studying the complicated, formal color theories. If you can understand how to work with value relationships (contrast in lightness and darkness of color), and if you understand the importance of intensity (or "chroma"—what to make brighter and what to make duller) you will be successful.

Color Terminology

Hue is another word for the name of a color.

Color is described in terms of value (the lightness or darkness of a color) and saturation, which is also known as intensity or chroma (the degree to which colors have been diluted).

Shade is the addition of black to a hue.

Tint is the addition of white to a hue.

Antique Bargello Inch Mat, 26" x 51", wool strips on burlap. Designer, artist, and date completed unknown. From the collection of Gail Dufresne. The neutral brown in this rug eases the transitions between the red, blue, and lavender colors.

Tone is the addition of gray to a hue.

Primary colors are the purest, most brilliant colors, not saturated by any other color. There are three primary colors: red, yellow, and blue.

Secondary colors are the result of combining two primary colors. There are three secondary colors: orange, green, and purple. The secondary colors, by definition, are not as pure or saturated as the primary colors. My favorite colors are orange, green, and purple, so I prefer to work with them.

Tertiary colors are produced when a primary and a secondary color are combined. They are red-orange, yellow-orange, yellow-green, blue-green, blue-purple, and red-purple.

Warm and cold colors. Warm colors are those in the red, orange, and yellow families. Cold colors are those in the blue, green, and purple families. Any color can be described as warm or cold. A color is warm if it is mixed with yellow, or cold if it is mixed with blue.

Classic Color Schemes

You do not have to memorize color schemes to work with color. You only need to know that they

Traditional Sunflower Inch Mat, 24" x 46", wool on linen. Designed and hooked by Gail Dufresne, Lambertville, New Jersey, 2003. Black and white throughout this rug provide a resting place for the eye.

exist for your use. If you have a basic color wheel, this information will always be at your disposal. Keep a color wheel as part of your essential rug hooking supplies so that you can refer to it whenever you need to.

Monochromatic color scheme. A monochromatic color scheme uses variations of lightness and brightness of a single color. The primary color can be integrated with neutrals such as black, white, or gray. The challenge here is to highlight the most important elements, and the key is to use several different values and levels of intensity of that color to enhance and add interest to the scheme.

Analogous color scheme. An analogous color scheme uses colors that are adjacent to each other on the color wheel. One color is used as the dominant color, while the others are used to enrich the scheme.

Complementary color scheme. A complementary color scheme is made up of two colors that are opposite each other on the color wheel. The complement of a primary color is the mixture of the other two primary colors. The complement of red, for example, is yellow and blue mixed together, or green. This scheme offers the strongest contrast of any color scheme. Usually one color is more predominately used and the other is used as an accent. Dyeing wool with a complementary color will dull it, but hooking one color next to its complement will intensify both colors.

Split complementary color scheme. A split complementary color scheme uses a color and the two colors on either side of the complementary color, such as red with yellow-green and blue-green.

Triadic color scheme. A triadic color scheme uses three colors equally spaced around the color wheel. It offers strong visual contrast while retaining balance and richness, but it is not as contrasting as the complementary scheme. A primary triad is red, yellow, and blue. The secondary triad uses green, orange, and purple. I most often work in a secondary color scheme.

McGown Friendship Mat, 17" x 51", various cuts of wool on linen, Designed Gail Dufresne, hooked by various artists, 2005. A double row of hooking adds interest to grid lines.

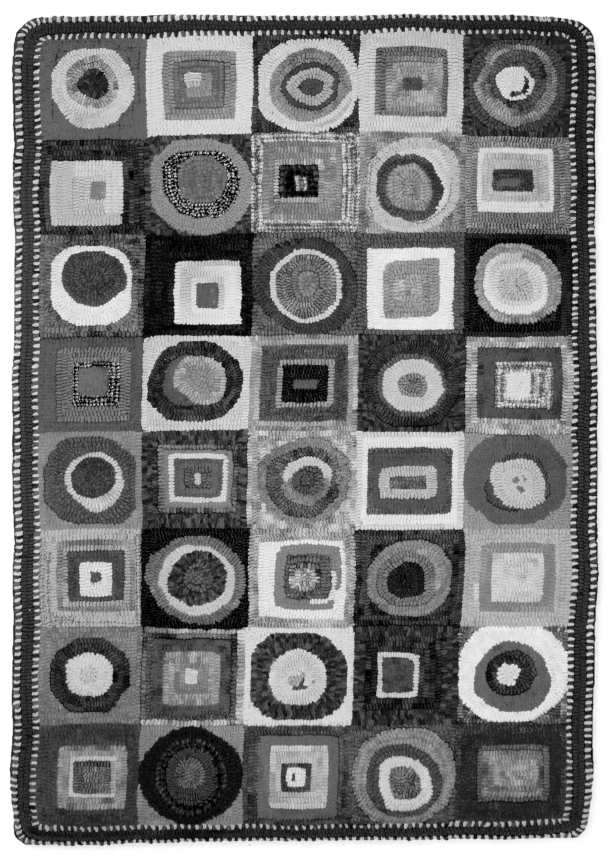

Evelyn's Geometric, 24" x 37", #7-cut on monk's cloth. Designed by Bev Conway. Hooked by Corinne Watts, Washington, DC, 2002. Grid lines can be eliminated for an informal, less structured look.

Achromatic color scheme. Technically not a color scheme, this arrangement uses no color, only black, white, and gray. The highest contrast possible is that between black and white. This scheme can create a vintage look or a bold, modern look. M. C. Escher is well known for his surrealistic black and white drawings.

Neutrals

Black, white, gray, and brown are considered neutrals. Browns are combinations of complementary colors and often have a cast of a particular color. If you pull out some brown wools and put them side by side—remember, this is all a game of relativity—you will see that some have a red cast, some a blue cast, some a green cast. Blacks may also have a warm or cool cast. *Smoke and Mirrors,* page 56, is an example of a piece that uses only neutrals.

Consider how neutrals work with other colors. They can enhance or play down other colors. You can successfully use unrelated colors if neutrals are mixed in with them, even to the extent of hooking every other row in a neutral. Neutrals can be a way to transition from color to color and motif to motif. The only colors used in an antique inch mat that I bought on eBay, page 45, are red, blue, and a little lavender, which may have been blue before it faded. Those colors next to each other would be nowhere near as pleasing as when they are separated by many different values of brown, which create interesting transitions and a wonderfully pleasing rug.

Buller, 16" x 16", #3- to 6-cut wool on rug warp. Designed and hooked by Mary Jane Whitelaw, Belle Mead, New Jersey, 2002. The background of this rug is two different values of green. The grid lines are the darker value of green.

Proddy Rooster, 18" x 20", #3- to 1/2"-cut wool on linen. Designed and hooked by Gail Dufresne, Lambertville, New Jersey, 2004.

I used all of the colors in the rooster's tail for my grid lines. This technique makes your eyes dance around the design, making this small piece seem larger than it really is.

General Sturgeon, 20" x 80", #7- and 8-cut wool on monk's cloth. Designed and hooked by Carol Feeny, Bonita Springs, Florida, 2008.

Don't ever count out pure black and white! Black and white provide a place for the eye to go after scanning and dancing around a myriad of colors. Black and white "contain" the colors, keeping them from running into nothingness or from becoming too much to look at. Black and white are a great choice for borders and other high-contrast spots. This combination stops the whole design from falling off into chaos and can add the final necessary element. It can represent the one constant—a return to order—in a sea of ever-changing color. Black and white do not compete with the rest of the colors. Use black and white together to give your work a punch.

MANAGING A COLOR PLAN

Students often ask me to color plan their entire rug before they even begin to hook. I applaud anyone who can do this on a regular basis! I just do not think it is possible (or necessary) to come up with a really good color plan before you even begin. There is no way we can really know how colors will play against each other before we see how they actually interact, before we hook a few loops side by side.

When I sit down to work on a new design, I rarely pre-plan the whole rug. I consider one square at a time. I strive to put as much creativity into that one square as I would the entire rug. Then I move on to the next square. I try to make it different than the first. I may decide that I need a particular, specific unifying order. For example, I might use one material throughout, or if it is a log cabin design, I may make all the chimneys the same color.

My design strategy breaks the rug hooking "rule" that states that you must start in the middle of the rug and work toward the outer edge. I suspect that this rule came about to ensure that those of us who hook very tight do not hook all around the center, making it bunch up so badly that it cannot be steamed down or, worse yet, cause the weak fibers of the foundation to break.

My method? I usually start at the element I know best and work toward the least known elements, regardless of where they are positioned. As I work the rug, it "tells" me where it wants to go and then the pieces fall into place. Remember, you may not like a piece until you're well into the hooking, so don't give up too early!

Use Lines to Your Advantage

Watch for every opportunity to play colors against each other. Every line in a design has the potential of adding interest, and should be used to best advantage. Many people give little thought to color planning grid lines, for instance. But grid lines are an integral part of the design, as important as any other line in that design. They do not always have to be black. In fact, they do not have to always be dark. A grid line simply gives you another place to "hang" color. Take advantage of the opportunity to add interest.

Cindy Macmillan found a way to use all of the pretty middle values that most of us prefer in her blocks of *Intervening Leaf Design*, page 5. She linked them with a very light-valued textured grid line. This color choice lightens the color scheme and allows the darker wools to shine individually rather than all meshing together.

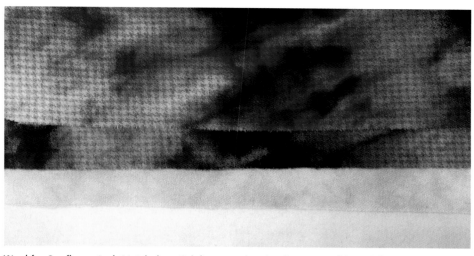

Wool for *Sunflower Inch Mat*, below. Rainbow wool makes for eye catching gridlines.
DAN SMITH PHOTOGRAPHY

Sunflower Inch Mat, 21" x 24", wool on linen. Designed and hooked by Gail Dufresne, Lambertville, New Jersey, 2000.
The grid lines in this rug vary in color by direction: off-white, dull yellow, and rainbow.

Consider these grid line variations:

- Hook double rows for the grid lines. I used two rows of a texture cut in a #8 for my *McGown Friendship Mat,* page 47.
- Eliminate either the vertical or horizontal grid lines. Corinne Watts did not hook the grid lines of *Evelyn's Geometric,* page 48.
- Try complementary colors, neutrals, or lighter or darker values of the colors in the piece. Mary Jean Whitelaw used two values of green for her background of *Buller,* page 49, a darker green in each square that surrounds the dog and a lighter green for the rest of the squares. She used the darker green to hook her grid lines so that they are the same color as the squares right around the dog. The lines disappear so they do not detract from Buller, who should be the star of the show.
- Use one color for the vertical grid lines and another value of that color—or another color entirely—for the horizontal grid lines. All of the colors in the rooster's tail were used for the grid lines in *Proddy Rooster,* page 49.

- Use wool that has been dip dyed with all of the colors in the design. In my *Sunflower Inch Mat,* page 51, I wanted to emphasize the traditional diamond, with intense contrasting colors radiating out from the sunflower. So I hooked the grid lines in three different colors: The lines running in one direction are off-white, and the lines running in the other direction alternate between a dull yellow and a dip-dyed wool that includes all the colors in the rainbow. This combination ensured that all the colors were evenly distributed around the rug.

We have other lines in our rugs. Borders are another type of line to color plan. The dip-dyed wool in *Sunflower Inch Mat* was a great choice for a "beauty line," the line between the background and border.

- One of my favorite ways to hook lines is to bead two colors together. Hold two strips of wool beneath the rug just as you would hold one. Pull a loop up from one color, then with your hook pull the other piece of wool around the first piece and pull up a loop of the second color. Continue alternating colors for a crisp, eye-catching line.

Antique Geometric, 28" x 42", wool on burlap. Designer, artist, and date completed unknown.
From the collection of Cindy Macmillan.

Circle Mosaic, 26" x 37 ¹/₂", #4- and 6-cut wool on monk's cloth. Designed and hooked by Patty Mahaffey, Perkasie, Pennsylvania, 2009. Repetitive designs featuring repeating colors make effective geometric rug designs.

Stars and Leaves, 31" x 21 $^1/_2$", #4- and 6-cut wool on monk's cloth. Designed by Cherylyn Brubaker. Hooked by Patty Mahaffey, Perkasie, Pennsylvania, 2010.

    Repeating designs that use the same colors in different positions add interest to this geometric rug.

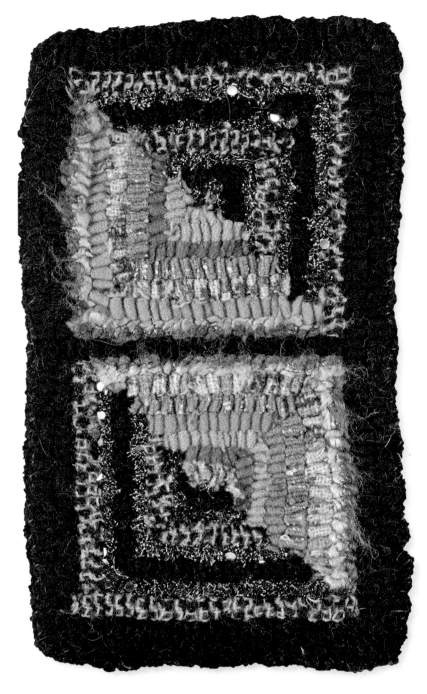

Smoke and Mirrors, 5" x 10", wool and other materials on linen. Designed and hooked by Gail Dufresne, Lambertville, New Jersey, 2005.

Neutrals include blacks, grays, whites, and browns. Neutrals can have a warm or cool cast and add interest to a hooked design.

Avoid Arbitrary Limits

Many students feel that there must be three and only three colors used in a rug. Where did this rule come from? For that matter, where does one color begin and another end? At what point does blue-green become true green? Think more in terms of having lots of values of whatever colors you do use. But use one color or 100 colors—it is your choice.

Strive for Repetition

Repeating shapes, lines, and colors—repetition unifies and strengthens a design as it ties together otherwise separate parts. The simple decision to color all the chimneys of a log cabin rug red creates harmony, order, and consistency throughout the rug. *Antique Geometric,* page 53, is a great example of the power of repetition. Patty Mahaffey's *Circle Mosaic,* page 54, was inspired by a piece of fabric. Patty repeated the same colors in each section and in the same position. Her rug *Stars and Leaves,* page 55, is also a simple repeating design. Although she used the same colors in each repeated motif, the colors are in different positions.

Above all else, trust yourself and have fun! You know better than anyone else what colors attract you and which colors make you happy. You can appreciate the work of others and their color palettes without having to adopt them as your own.

When I am holding colors in my hand that make my heart sing, life feels good. You will never be happy using colors that do not appeal to you. The most unhappy students I encounter are those who are trying to work outside of their own color preferences or are making a rug for someone else and trying to figure out what the other person likes. I am not saying that you should not make rugs for others, but when you are making one for yourself, be confident and trust your color instincts. You are choosing to make rugs—no one is making you do it. It should be fun!

CHAPTER FOUR

Creating a Three-Dimensional Geometric Design
Perspective, Sculpting, and Prodding

I will probably never hook another rug that does not incorporate some technique that gives the rug a more three-dimensional look. It is yet another reason why I am naturally drawn to geometric designs, which are so easily manipulated to incorporate three-dimensional elements.

PERSPECTIVE

Perspective is a three-dimensional illusion in a two-dimensional subject or space. You can achieve the look of depth and volume by using devices that trick viewers into seeing an optical illusion, making them forget that they are seeing a flat picture. With effective use of these

Little Sheepish, 18" x 18", #3- to 8-cut wool on linen. Designed and hooked by Gail Dufresne, Lambertville, New Jersey, 2002.
This curious sheep looks as though he is sitting in front of the background inch squares. I grounded him by tucking him into the background squares at his base so it appears as though he is peeking out of a window of squares.

Barn Raising Log Cabin, 28" x 40", #5- and 7-cut wool on linen. Designed by Gail Dufresne. Hooked by Barbara Kimbrough, Wall, New Jersey, 2010. A three-dimensional illusion can be achieved by clever use of colors and values, as in many log cabin designs.

Log Cabin, 28" x 40", #6-cut wool on linen. Designed and hooked by Cindy Macmillan, Newtown, Pennsylvania, 2004. By manipulating the placement of values, Cindy created a crisp optical illusion where the lighter diamonds appear to float over the darker squares.

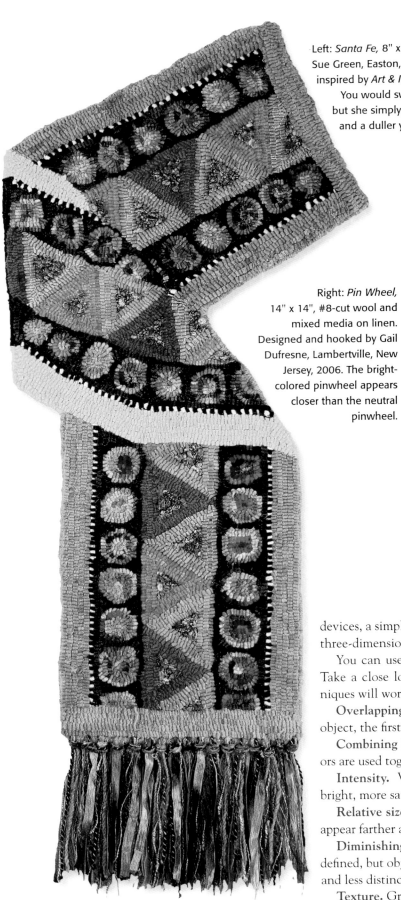

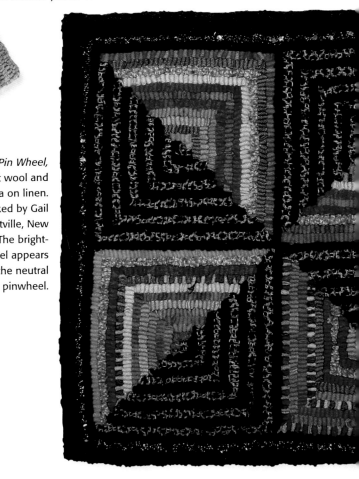

Left: *Santa Fe,* 8" x 32", #6-cut wool on linen. Designed and hooked by Sue Green, Easton, Maryland, 2009. Black and white border design inspired by *Art & Inspirations* by Yvonne Porcella.

You would swear that Sue Green's *Santa Fe* is actually folded over, but she simply used a bright yellow on the front section of the border and a duller yellow on the back border.

Right: *Pin Wheel,* 14" x 14", #8-cut wool and mixed media on linen. Designed and hooked by Gail Dufresne, Lambertville, New Jersey, 2006. The bright-colored pinwheel appears closer than the neutral pinwheel.

devices, a simple two-dimensional repeating design can become a three-dimensional work of art.

You can use more than one of these techniques in one rug. Take a close look at these creative rugs. Which of these techniques will work with the geometric design you have planned?

Overlapping motifs. If one object covers a part of a second object, the first object appears closer.

Combining lights and darks. When light colors and dark colors are used together, light colors advance and dark colors recede.

Intensity. When brights and dulls are used together, the bright, more saturated colors advance and the dull colors recede.

Relative size. Larger objects appear closer, and smaller objects appear farther away.

Diminishing detail. Close objects appear sharp and clearly defined, but objects farther away appear blurred, lacking in detail, and less distinct.

Texture. Greater, more defined textures advance, while lighter textures recede.

Queen Anne, 30" x 48", #5-cut wool on linen. Designed by Heirloom. Hooked by Cathy Edwards, Salem, South Carolina, 2009. In Cathy's geometric, the bright pink flowers appear to float in front of the rest of the rug.

Echo, 28" x 44", #6-cut wool on burlap. Designed by Jane McGown Flynn. Hooked by Corinne Watts, Washington, DC, 2008.

    The warm colors in this simple repeat design catch our eye and guide us right to the center of the rug.

Abyss, 25" x 35", #2- to 7-cut wool on burlap. Adapted from a color plate in a Dover Publication book and hooked by Corinne Watts, Washington, DC, 2008.

This rug is another example of effective use of warm and cool colors. The warm colors at the center pull the viewer right into the abyss—as do the diagonal black lines.

Kentucky Montage, 36" x 50", #8- to 10-cut wool on linen. Designed by Melissa Elliott. Hooked by Cynthia Norwood, Kirtland, Ohio, 2009.

The border of this rug uses quilt motifs to reflect the strong quilting heritage of the state. Quilt designs are often geometric designs. These squares, circles, and rectangles provide an opportunitiy to play with color and value.

Tribute to Vasarely, 13" x 13", #5- to #8-cut wool on linen. Designed and hooked by Gail Dufresne, Lambertville, New Jersey, 2007.

I hooked the center square of this rug in a #8 cut and hooked each row of squares out to the edge in a progressively smaller cut. The design appears to be rounded, with the center being closest to the viewer. The heavier texture of a wider cut (as well as the progressively duller colors out to the edge and the angle of the grid lines) creates the optical illusion.

Above: *Mary Jean's Corvette,*
27" x 36", #3- to 8-cut wool and
roving on linen. Designed and
hooked by Mary Jean Whitelaw,
Belle Mead, New Jersey, 2009.

Mary Jean's husband's Corvette
appears to be speeding by her
house. She accomplished this trick
of perspective by using very grayed
material in the background and
breaking up the precise, angular
lines of the house.

Left: *Big Sheepish,* 18" x 20", #3-
to 8-cut wool and wool boucles on
linen. Designed and hooked by
Gail Dufresne, Lambertville, New
Jersey, 2002.

I enjoy working with boucles
(the fibers are actually twisted
around each other) and other
coarse textures that work well for
hooking animals. I usually don't
care if a material is 100% wool, as
long as it gives me the effect I am
trying to achieve.

CREATING A THREE-DIMENSIONAL GEOMETRIC DESIGN ■ 65

Purple Mixed Mania, 30" x 42", #3- to 8-cut wool and various natural and manmade fabrics. Designed and hooked by Gail Dufresne, Lambertville, New Jersey, 2009.

I used several other fabrics in addition to wool, including some wonderful velvet. I hooked much of this rug, but I also embellished it by sewing on and weaving in velvets, ribbons, sequined material, and all sorts of great looking fibers.

Closeup of a lizard on *Lizards and Ladders.* (See the full rug on page ii.)

Sculpting adds dimension to a rug. The gecko appears to be walking across this gameboard.

Incorporating Mixed Media

I had the once-in-a-lifetime opportunity to teach at the Reeth Rug Retreat in England, where I learned as much as I taught. In England, the cost of wool is so prohibitive that the rug makers rarely use off-the-bolt wool for their projects. They use recycled wool, yarns, scraps of fabric such as velvet—even plastic bags. They work much like the first rug makers did, using whatever they have on hand. They design their own rugs since there are few pattern makers in England and readymade designs are so expensive. Lest you think that their work is not on par with ours, think again! What they create with what they have is amazing, and may make you think twice about assuming that you have to use only 100% wool in your work.

I have included yarns and other mixed media fibers in my work for a number of years now. I find that mixed media lends a wonderful three-dimensional effect to a hooked rug, even without employing the tricks demonstrated earlier. I am not sure that I will ever hook another flat, two-dimensional piece again, and since I don't think any of my work will ever be meant for the floor, I don't have to worry about whether the materials I use will wear well underfoot. If you decide to use mixed media in your work, however, you will have to carefully consider where you want to place the finished rug as you design, color plan, and choose materials.

If the mixed media materials you choose are very heavy or look like they might not be something that will run through a cutter, try using a handheld rotary cutter. I also take care when I am steaming my work, as some fibers, such as polyester, melt at a much lower temperature than wool.

Purple Mixed Mania uses all sorts of gems from my purple wool basket. That basket is where I toss everything purple: textured and solid wools, both as is and overdyed; purple silk; purple yarns…. I keep this basket on hand near my hooking chair and use it for most of my projects. I have become quite partial to purple!

I actually sewed materials onto *Purple Mixed Mania* to give it even more dimension. I used lots of different bits of velvet given to me by one of my English students who lived near a velvet factory in England. She had accumulated so much

velvet that she had a separate storage area on her property to house it all!

In addition to using any materials I can get my hands on—especially if they are bright, glitzy, or glittery—I also regularly sculpt and prod to create a three-dimensional look.

SCULPTING

Sometimes called "Waldoboro," named for a town in Maine, these rugs are known for their deep pile, which is clipped and sculpted to make specific design elements stand out from the background.

In order to sculpt, you will need a very sharp pair of scissors to cut and contour your loops to the desired shape. A brush to get out the loose fluff after clipping is desirable but not necessary. Fuller Brush makes a great hairbrush cleaner tool that is perfect for this step, but a soft toothbrush will work just as well.

The size of the motif that you intend to sculpt as well as the desired look for the sculpted motif will determine the cut of wool that you hook it with. If an area is very small, a small cut may be best. For example, for a finely shaded flower you

Detail from *Traditional Sunflower Inch Mat*, page 46.

Sculpting works especially well for flowers. Hooks prod and sculpt the petals and centers using different techniques to add interest to your piece. IMPACT XPOZURES may want a smooth, velvety effect, so you should use a smaller cut. If you want to sculpt something like a funky chicken wing, however, you may need to need a wider cut so you can leave the loops jagged and rough.

Begin hooking at the low edge of the section to be sculpted. Pull the loops as you normally would, to the height of the loop width. Hook into every hole. This is one time where packing is a good thing! Pull each successive row progressively higher until the high point of the sculpture is reached—the top of a lizard's head or the middle of the sunflower center, for example. If the loops are pulled just a little higher than the previous row you will not have to clip off as much excess wool.

The most important thing to remember when you're sculpting is "think high!" Don't be timid about pulling up the loops. After all, what you are after is a third dimension—height.

After completing a section, remove your piece from the frame or hoop, then clip and carve the wool to produce the effect you want. I often start by just shaving over the top of the motif, then I go back and clip each loop. Brush or shake off loose bits of wool so you can see the three-dimensional effect more clearly. If you get carried away and clip too much or decide that you want the area to be higher, simply hook in more loops and begin the clipping process again.

PRODDING

Prodded rugs are made from long strips of fabric poked through a backing. The effect is similar to that of hooked rugs, but the technique produces a rug with a longer, shaggier pile. More common in Great Britain than in North America, prodded rugs are known by various names in different communities: "poked" and "proggie" are some common terms.

Prodded designs are often—but certainly not always—simpler than hooked rug designs because the longer pile makes details difficult. For the gardeners among you, fluffy hollyhock, delphinium, and lupine flowerets or big, loose roses translate easier than flatter, more one-dimensional flowers such as violets and pansies. Prodding moves along much faster than rug hooking, so your piece is finished sooner, and who does not like such immediate gratification?

Any weight wool can be used for prodded rugs. I prefer heavier coat-weight wool or wool that I have felted (often by mistake) as it is stiffer and stands up better. Coat-weight wool is usually cheaper than rug hooking–weight wool, and it is also easier to trim. All sorts of yarns, mohair, and non-wool material are wonderful to experiment with.

STEAMING

Ideally, it is best to complete the hooking before you begin sculpting or prodding so that the hooking can be steamed before those elements are added. If a prodded or sculpted area gets really tight, I lay my mat on a table and really stretch it with my hands to flatten it out. Linen is very strong and can take this abuse.

Avoid steaming if you've used any sort of mixed medium that will not tolerate steam—either its heat or its moisture. I once added so much extra material to my mat that the sides did not lay flat, so I decided to steam it. The finished piece did come out well once it dried, but wet, dripping strips of mohair and yarn are not a pretty sight. I don't recommend steaming it if you can avoid it.

Geometric Floral Proddy, 36" x 48", #4-cut to ¹/₂" torn wool on linen, Designed and hooked by Yvonne Wood, Somers, Connecticut, 2000.

Yvonne started this wonderful geo-floral rug in a geometric design class. When boredom hit, she decided to prod flowers at the bottom to make the original geometric design look like an elaborate garden wall.

CHAPTER FIVE

Backgrounds and Borders
Simple or Elaborate

Road Kill, 8" x 8", #8-cut wool on linen. Designed and hooked by Gail Dufresne, Lambertville, New Jersey, 2008. This unfortunate critter is superimposed over an inch mat grid with unexpected colors and shapes.

When we decide what motif, or subject, we want to hook—a sheep, a bowl of fruit, flowers—we often don't consider how we want to treat the empty, negative space around the subject. This negative space is our background, and it is vitally important to the rug. If we do not want to put our sheep into a realistic landscape setting, for example, what are our options—what kind of a background do we want? After we make that decision, another question arises—should we add a border? If we decide on a border, what type of border will be most effective? These decisions can make or break a rug.

GEOMETRIC BACKGROUNDS

Negative space is the space around and between the subject(s) of an image. The use of negative space is a key element of artistic composition. Why is it that even though our rugs may contain more negative space, or background, than subject matter, we give it the least amount of thought? Consider the background in your rug as an opportunity for even more fun.

When I first started hooking back in 1984, we all hated to hook backgrounds. We tried hard to hook them a little at a time as we went along, in between hooking the more fun and much more interesting and colorful motifs. Back then, even if the rug was a room-sized

Howdy, 38¹/₂" x 45", #6-cut wool on linen. Designed by Gail Dufresne. Hooked by Gail Schmidt, Little Silver, New Jersey, 2008.

A busy geometric background focuses attention on the cowboy. Geometric backgrounds do not have to be symmetrical or repetitious. Note the many shapes and sizes of rectangles and squares.

Geometric Pot Pourri, #3-cut to 8-cut wool on burlap. Designed by Jane McGown Flynn. Hooked by Gail Dufresne, Lambertville, New Jersey, 1996.

I added a long lizard to cover up some of the background in this intricate geometric rug.

masterpiece, the entire background was usually hooked with one wool, which was most likely one solid flat color, like maroon, eggplant, celery, ecru, or navy blue. Backgrounds couldn't be too flashy. We might wash the wool to fluff it up a little or simmer it in a pot of water with some detergent for a little mottling. The tedium of hooking the majority of the rug in just one monotonous color often made us toss the piece into our piles of undone projects so that we could move on to something more interesting.

Times have changed and so have hooked rugs. While we do not want our backgrounds to overpower our motifs, they certainly do not have to be a vast sea of one flat color!

In a composition, the background space around an object is just as important as the object itself. By using geometric backgrounds, many of which can easily stand on their own, I am able to create interesting and ever changing color plays and shapes in the spaces among and around my main motifs.

I hooked my first geometric in 1996, a Jane McGown Flynn design called *Geometric Pot Pourri*, which I was required to complete in order to earn my McGown teacher's certification. The pattern was comprised of 40 blocks, each a 5" square, and I had a terrible time developing a pleasing and cohesive color scheme. Hooking a bunch of seemingly unrelated squares seemed beyond tedious. One day, I happened to be wearing my favorite lizard T-shirt, a memento from a trip to Belize. I suddenly had an idea. What if I spread a lizard diagonally across the rug? That lizard would hide many of those squares that I did not know what to do with and make the rug so much more fun to hook. My *Geometric Pot Pourri* was the result.

Goat Hill, page 26, is one of my favorite designs. Ruby Pearl proudly stands in front of a very bold background that was adapted from a Kaffe Fassett design. He is hooked in all neutrals— brown, black, white, and gray. He covers the squares behind him so he seems to stand out in front of the background.

Mary Jean's Sheep Rug, 25" x 34", #8-cut wool on linen. Designed by DiFranza. Hooked by Mary Jean Whitelaw, Belle Mead, New Jersey, 1999. A simple border works hard to fence in Mary Jean's sheep.

Ms. Moo, 33" x 45", #6-cut wool on burlap. Designed by Morton House. Hooked by Gail Dufresne, Lambertville, New Jersey, 1992. I hooked this border to keep the cow in her pasture, but you'll notice her ear is escaping on the left.

MJ's Maverick, 30" x 30", #8-cut wool on linen. Designed and hooked by Mary Jean Whitelaw, Belle Mead, New Jersey, 2009.

Mary Jean's horse breaks the border, which mimics the colors of a corral and the grass beyond.

As you begin a rug, you don't need to know the actual colors you will use in your background, but you should know what *values* you will use so that the contrast between the motifs and the background will work. Dark motifs will work on medium or light value backgrounds, for example, but they will get lost on dark backgrounds. Make value decisions in the beginning and you'll save yourself hours of reverse hooking (pulling out your work) later.

GEOMETRIC BORDERS

If you do not want to hook an entire geometric rug, you can hook just a geometric border. Geometric borders contain the design and give it a defined stopping place

without detracting from the main subject matter.

Border possibilities are endless. They can be simple or very elaborate, but they should relate somehow to the design—or at least not detract from it. Don't just add a border on your rug because you feel that you are supposed to. You could end up with a border that is totally unrelated to the rug and looks like it was merely slapped on to fill space. Be certain that the border is an integral part of your rug. Mary Jean Whitelaw's cute sheep are nicely fenced in with a simple linear border that is a perfect ending to this rug. Likewise, Ms. Moo is not going to be able to walk out of her pasture into harm's way.

Melissa Elliott designed *Kentucky Montage* for three artists with very different styles to show how each would interpret the same design. The rug is made up of motifs that reflect the history of Kentucky. This geometric border is comprised of quilt blocks strung together, paying homage to the state's rich arts and crafts history. I flew through the interior of the design, hooking away, inspired and having fun. But I hit a total block when I got to the border. I stared at it for hours. . . days. . . weeks. . . not knowing how to treat the very busy border in a way that was exciting but did not detract from the rest of the rug. (I did indeed think of eliminating it!) I finally settled on using the colors of the painted sky and, of course, a little glitz. Pulling out any more colors from the center would have been just too distracting. This might seem to be a wild border to some, but it was in keeping with the style of my rug.

Choosing Border Colors

The general rule when creating borders is to make them darker and duller than the rest of the rug. A great example of this is *Log Cabin Spin*. Notice how the grayed inner border is made up of medium and dark valued wools. The outer border is composed of several rows of solid black wool and one line of the bright red wool

Kentucky Montage, 27" x 36", #3- to 8-cut wool and yarn on linen. Designed by Melissa Elliott. Hooked by Gail Dufresne, Lamberville, New Jersey, 2010.

The border picks up the colors in the sky, resulting in a satisfying geometric border surrounding the busy interior.

Compare this with the two other *Kentucky Montage* rugs to see how three different artists interpreted the same design (pages 41 and 64).

Closeup of *Log Cabin Spin*. A duller border carries on the brighter colors of the inner rug. (See the full rug on page 30.)

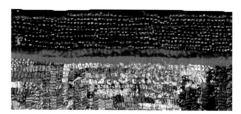

Closeup of *Zig Zag Log Cabin.* The edge of this rug mirrors its red beauty line. (See the full rug on page 34.)

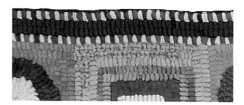

Closeup of *Evelyn's Geometric.* The edge of this rug features rows of beading on either side of vibrant green wool. (See the full rug on page 48.)

Leavy Antique, 28" x 47", #6-cut wool on linen. Designed by Hook Nook. Hooked by Gail Dufresne, Lambertville, New Jersey, 1995.

Border colors are often chosen to reflect the colors used in a rug's motif.

found in the center of each block. I did not place the bright red line exactly in the middle of the border, but hooked a different number of black rows on either side of it.

Solid black, however, is not always a good choice for borders. I used it for the *Log Cabin Spin* border because I had used solid black within the rug. In many instances, however, black may be too dark and heavy, detracting from the rest of the rug.

On *Zig Zag Log Cabin,* I used the same border technique, but since this was meant to be a low contrast rug, I hooked one line of a transitional red-and-black

houndstooth wool between the bright red wool from the centers and the black textured wool that I used for the rest of the border.

An example of a great border wool that is not darker and duller than the wool used in the rest of the rug is Corinne Watts' *Evelyn's Geometric,* in which she banded two rows of a vibrant green wool with a row of beading.

In my version of *Leavy Antique,* an inner border reflects the wild colors used in the inner rug. I hooked a 1" border of dark purple outside that inner border to calm the rug down. I am not sure I was

Left: Closeup of *Stars and Leaves.* The edge of this rug mirrors its red beauty line. (See the full rug on page 55.)

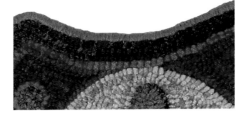

Left: Closeup of *Lizards and Ladders.* Busy borders don't have to distract from a geometric rug. (See the full rug on page ii.)

Closeup of *Echo.* A sculpted border allowed the artist to complete the shapes along the edge instead of cropping them. (See the full rug on page 62.)

successful at doing that, but I still like those wild, swirling bands of color!

As a general rule, avoid using a color in the border that you have not used elsewhere in your rug. The color you use in the border will make that same color stand out elsewhere in the rug. It sends the viewer's eyes into the rug, looking for that same color.

In *Intervening Leaf Design*, Cindy Macmillan chose one of the darker textured wools used in her rug for the border.

She then whipstitched the rug with yarn that was close in color to that textured wool. The result is a plain but handsome and effective border that sets off and complements the rest of the rug.

Plaids and patterned wool are great to use as borders, but only if the colors of the fabric are also used in the inner part of the rug. For example, using a colorful plaid wool in the border of a rug that uses the individual colors in the plaid can be wonderfully effective.

Mary Jean's Log Cabin, 26" x 38", #8-cut wool on linen. Designed and hooked by Mary Jean Whitelaw, Belle Mead, New Jersey, 2003.

This border gives Mary Jean's rug a complete three-dimensional look.

Shaped Borders

Your border does not have to be a straight line. In Patty Mahaffey's rug *Stars and Leaves,* the line of the finished edge mirrors the design's red beauty line.

You may choose a shaped border to help complete the shapes in a geometric rug. When Corinne Watts finished hooking *Echo* as it was designed, she wasn't satisfied. The rug seemed incomplete since the border line cut through the design and left half-circles along the edge. Those half-circles bothered her, so she decided to complete the circles by adding the other halves, which then created an irregular edge of scallops and points.

Think Outside the Box

A border can be incredibly detailed and complex as long as it matches the rest of the rug. Mary Jean Whitelaw's brilliantly conceived log cabin border gives her rug even more of a three-dimensional look than she had already achieved.

Same Border, Different Look

Let's take a look at the same design hooked with different borders. Patty Mahaffey beaded one row of black and white, then hooked the border of *Twilight Zone* with the same black wool she used for the background. Allie Barchi completed her *Twilight Zone* with a two-toned border, which allowed her to pull two colors out from the main rug.

Often, two of my prolific students choose the same design, but each put their own spin on it. The results are always fascinating. Corinne Watts hooked the border of Melissa Elliot's design *Kaleidoscope* as it was drawn, where the central motifs appear to be behind the border motifs. Patty Mahaffey simplified that border, giving the same pattern a whole new twist.

How about the same rug, with and without a border? Allie Barchi hooked *Cosmic Highway* with all sorts of cool materials, including a shimmery background wool that stands on its own. The finished rug doesn't need a border—or anything else! Sue Green's version of

Twilight Zone, 21" x 23", #4- and 6-cut wool on monk's cloth. Designed by Go Primitive, Lisa Livingston. Hooked by Patty Mahaffey, Perkasie, Pennsylvania, 2008.

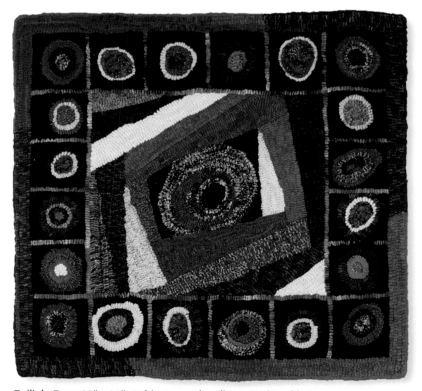

Twilight Zone, 22" x 23", #8^1/$_2$-cut wool on linen. Designed by Go Primitive, Lisa Livingston. Hooked by Allie Barchi, Malvern, Pennsylvania, 2008

Kaleidoscope, 30" x 40", #4- and 6-cut wool on monk's cloth. Designed by Melissa Elliott. Hooked by Patty Mahaffey, Perkasie, Pennsylvania, 2005.

Kaleidoscope, 30" x 40", #4- and 6-cut wool on monk's cloth. Designed by Melissa Elliott. Hooked by Corinne Watts, Washington, DC, 2008.

Cosmic Highway, 31¹/₂" x 38¹/₂", #8¹/₂- and 9-cut wool and mixed media on linen. Designed by Main Street Rugs, Melissa Elliott. Hooked by Allie Barchi, Malvern, Pennsylvania, 2008.

A border is not always necessary, as seen here in Allie's shimmery rug.

Cosmic Highway, 36½" x 44½", wool and mixed media on linen. Designed by Main Street Rugs, Melissa Elliott. Hooked by Sue Green, Easton, Maryland, 2007.

Sue's liberal use of black and white is reminiscent of quilter Yvonne Porcella's work.

Southwest Memories, 8" x 24", #4- and 6-cut wool on linen. Designed and hooked by Sue Green, Easton, Maryland, 2006.

Black and white borders contain rugs beautifully and are an ideal choice for geometric rugs of any color, size, or shape.

Cosmic Highway, hooked with wool and yarns, is also a stunner. Her border is a knockout and is different both in content and width on all four sides.

Black and White Borders and Checkerboards

I adore black and white. Apparently my students do, too, as shown by the number of rugs I have with black and white borders. Black and white contain colors so well that they are an obvious and popular choice for borders. You can't go wrong with a basic black-and-white checkerboard border, but back and white can go beyond simple. Look at the grand border on Mary Jean Whitelaw's *Corvette*, page 65, where the squares mirror the black-and-white racing flag.

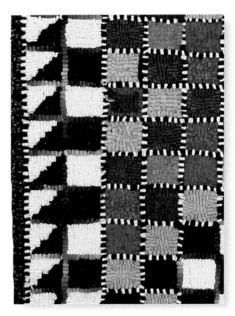

Closeup of *Traditional Sunflower Inch Mat.* Partial squares form another twist on the traditional checkerboard border. (See the full rug on page 46.)

Closeup of *Corvette*. The black and white border here reminds the viewer of a racing flag. (See the full rug on page 65.)

Pansy With Inch Mat Border, 18" x 18", wool on linen. Designed and hooked by Gail Dufresne, Lambertville, New Jersey, 2002. Basic checkerboards can combine any colors, such as the white and purple here.

Painted Tulip without border.

Checkerboard borders don't have to be black and white. Other colors work just as well, as in this pansy pillow border, right, where white wool and the dark purple wool of the pansy make up the checkerboard.

I used half black/half white squares for the border on my *Traditional Sunflower Inch Mat*. The center square is all black. I reversed the direction of the black and white hooking at the center point. I got this idea from my *Antique Traditional Inch Mat*.

What a Difference a Border Can Make

I hooked my *Painted Tulip* to teach my Wednesday students how to hook as though they are painting. I thought it looked fine without a border. But as an experiment, and as an example to demonstrate how borders change a rug, I worked up a simple geometric border using rectangles of black, white, and colors from the tulip. What a difference! I could not believe how much the border enhanced the piece! It gave the rug a bold punch yet did not detract from or

Painted Tulip, 26" by 31", #3-cut wool and yarn on linen. Designed and hooked by Gail Dufresne, Lambertville, New Jersey, 2010. IMPACT XPOZURES

compete with the tulip. It contains and completes the design.

Backgrounds and borders are so important, and there are an infinite number of ways to treat them. You may even decide that your rug does not need a border. There is no one right answer, and what

you choose may be totally different from what someone else would choose—but equally as effective. Take the time to sketch and color out a few possibilities before you decide, and then trust yourself to make the right choice for your design.

CHAPTER SIX

Abstraction
A Different Way to Design

For years I worked with geometrically structured designs primarily inspired by traditional gridded quilt designs. I learned much of what I know about design and color by studying and hooking them, but in the past few years I have grown less interested in these structured designs and felt that it was time for me to move on. Enough already! Now I want to explore work that does not rely on right-angled geometry. I am drawn to the abstract, work that is freed from the rigidity of templates and symmetry.

I have been studying and researching abstract artists; one of my favorites is Wassily Kandinsky. I recently had the opportunity to see his work at the Guggenheim Museum in New York City.

I was fascinated by his progression from easily recognizable, organic images to bold, exciting relationships between line, form, and color, his images becoming more and more abstract as time went on.

This progression vaguely reminded me of one of my own favorite pieces, *Chimera*, which I hooked years ago. As I study it now, I can see it as a progression into abstraction as shapes radiate out from the three recognizable mythological creatures in the center. Even though I loved this design when I hooked it, I was not ready to take the plunge into abstraction at that stage of my journey.

An incredibly accomplished and innovative quilter, Nancy Crow, has also taken this journey, which she writes about in her book *Nancy Crow*. She had also lost interest in the usual rectilinear and template processes of traditional Anglo-American quilting. She was inspired by, among others, the African-American quilt maker Anna Williams. Williams assembled small bits of material into long strips and then pieced them together into a whole quilt top. The term "spontaneous quilts" was coined to describe her method of spontaneously cutting and sewing without the traditional use of blocks and templates. Her work revolutionized the quilting world. (For an interview with Katherine Watts and Anna Williams, read *A Colourful Journey: Over Twenty Designs from*

ROWAN for Patchwork and Quilting). Crow also abandoned templates and began cutting shapes freehand, judging proportions instinctively by eye, and inventing her own curvilinear, irregular structures. The results are stunning, exciting, and groundbreaking.

CREATING AN ABSTRACT

Jean Wells, another quilter who was ready for something new, studied extensively with Nancy Crow. She writes about her journey in her book *Intuitive Color and Design: Adventures in Art Quilting*, in which she creates abstract designs from her daughter's photographs.

To explore the gradual, step-by-step process of taking an image from realism to abstraction, I asked Cindy Macmillan for a few of her photographs. I was drawn to a photo of a barn set behind railroad tracks. The lines of the rooftops and the barn overhang caught my eye and I was attracted to the colors. I could, with pleasure, hook this realistic image just as it appears in the photograph, but my goal was to learn the process of abstraction.

First I traced the photograph onto a piece of paper. Then I began to play around with particular lines. It was not easy for me to move my ideas from the actual photo—and a literal interpretation—to an abstract design. My tendency was to take the image literally, reproducing it as it stood, because that is what I have always done and it is how I think. It took many hours and many steps, but I carved out time for myself in the early morning, when I think most clearly, several days in a row. I truly loved the process and the creative zone this exercise brought me to.

I was happy and intrigued with what I developed, but I wanted to take the process further toward abstraction. I looked through my sketchbook and found a photo of an antique rug that reminded me of the roof lines in Cindy's photograph. Thinking about my journey toward abstraction, I adapted these lines into *Barn Abstraction*. The simple flowing lines can be color planned in any way and hooked in any cut. Hooked at the suggested size of

Chimera, 38" x 51", #3- to 5-cut wool on burlap. Designed by New Earth Designs. Hooked by Gail Dufresne, Lambertville, New Jersey, 1995. This rug is representative of a study of abstracts and the progression from the recognizable to the artist's interpretation.

My first attempt at creating an abstract design started with a photograph that captured my imagination.

This drawing shows one of my interim designs based on Cindy's barn photo.

Barn Abstraction, 18" x 24", mixed cuts of wool and yarn on linen. Designed and hooked by Gail Dufresne, Lambertville, New Jersey, 2010. For this abstract design, I chose wool to match the colors in the original photograph.

Grate 1, 18" x 26", #5-cut wool on linen. Designed and hooked by Sue Green, Easton, Maryland, 2006.

Something as simple as a metal grate can inspire a gorgeous rug.

14" x 21", a medium cut of wool will work well. But you can simply reduce or enlarge the design to the size that will accommodate the cut you wish to use.

I loved the colors in the photograph, so I knew that I would enjoy using them in my design. I chose a mixture of wool and yarns that mirrored those colors. We tend to miss the neutrals or odd colors that we think are not interesting, and I did just that when I first chose my materials. I overlooked the taupe and tan colors of the railroad tracks on my first pass.

Intrigued? If you'd like to take the leap to designing and color planning abstract rugs, pay close attention to your surroundings. Find something that really interests you. Analyze what attracts you—is it the color? The design? Inspiration can come from anywhere: magazines, architecture, a walk in the park, old photographs. If something catches your eye, such as a brick wall or the angle of a garden trellis, sketch or photograph it and keep it in your sketchbook so that you have it as a reference material from which to choose when you are looking for ideas.

The simplest, most mundane objects can grab us. Sue Green was inspired by a metal grate. In *Grate 1*, she created a design based on the lines of the grate that caught her eye.

In order to take the journey into abstraction, you will need to relax and embrace the process rather than focusing on the outcome. Give yourself time to make mistakes. Challenge yourself. Explore line, design, and color in new ways. The *process* is the journey, so embrace it—fearlessly.

If you constantly doubt yourself and the direction in which you are going, the journey will not be any fun. All artistic endeavors have their doubtful times—that's part of the process. You are navigating uncharted waters, and it can be scary. If you are not sure that your piece is working, either work to get a little farther along so you have more to evaluate, or stop and study what you have. Solving your own

Allie's Rug, 16¹/₂″ round, #6-cut wool and yarn bits on linen. Designed and hooked by Allie Barchi, Malvern, Pennsylvania, 2010.

Allie worked from a photograph her son had taken. The result is a great little round mat, and the colors truly reflect the mood of her son's photograph.

problems will make you grow artistically. It will force you to look for other ideas and solutions.

A wonderful way to get constructive feedback is to form a group of like-minded souls who want to experiment in new ways and take their work to a higher level. Brainstorming ideas with a group such as this is an invaluable way to get constructive feedback and to move you though the blocked times which come to us all.

Be open to change. Even if you start with a carefully thought-out plan, you do not have to stick with it. Go with your gut reaction and allow the work to evolve. The piece will eventually take on a life of its own, developing its own energy and propelling you all the way to the end.

THE DESIGN PROCESS

When you are ready to design, select a visual from your sketch book. You can either make a simple freehand drawing or trace the lines. Start small— you don't have to take on a huge design to learn this process. Don't try to draw or trace every line and shape. Simplify. You will not at this point know how it will work out, but just keep an open mind and let the piece develop as you work.

Think about whether you want to work with the whole design or just a portion of it. Crop the design with anything that allows you to section off different areas. You can construct window templates out of cardboard, or use two rulers to cordon off an area—anything that will help you isolate a specific area and focus on it.

The sky is the limit in creating your design. You can:

- Use the entire visual as it is.
- Use just a section of the visual.
- Compose a repeating design by twisting and turning a section that interests you.
- Divide the original visual into equal parts and then rearrange them. Jean Wells talks about an interesting design technique called "slice and dice." She traces or sketches a visual and divides it into blocks. Then she rearranges the blocks. The blocks can be separated and made into individual designs or gridded together in one design with rows of hooking.

Photograph that was the inspiration for Allie's rug, above.

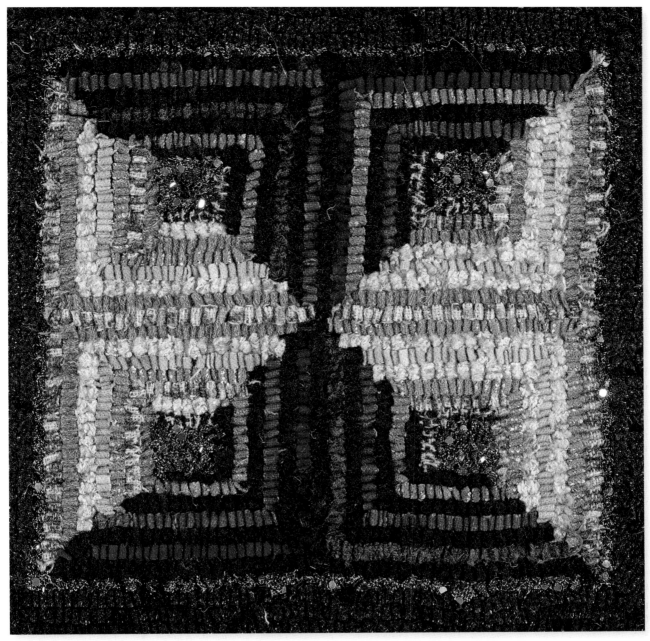

Abstract Log Cabin, 10" x 10", various materials on linen. Designed and hooked by Gail Dufresne, Lambertville, New Jersey, 2010.

FINAL THOUGHTS ON ABSTRACTIONS

It has taken me years and a lot of effort to get where I am today. Remember that creativity is a lifetime endeavor, and our creative ideas will grow, develop, and evolve through time. We must learn to go with that flow. We all have the same 24 hours a day. It is what we do with that time that makes the difference. Make a commitment to do something—anything— every day to get your creative juices flowing. Figure out what time of day you are the most creative and open, and carve out that time—even if it means that you

have to get up earlier or stay up later in the evening. You owe it to yourself.

You may be more comfortable starting your journey into design by using classic gridded quilt structures such as log cabin, courthouse steps, trip around the world, or nine patch. Different-size blocks such as those used for the background of *Goat Hill* might be another starting point. Simply draw out one of these quilt designs and use the colors found in your inspiration. From there, you can free yourself from the grids and rulers and create an abstract of your own.

Further Reading

- *A Colourful Journey: Over Twenty Designs from ROWAN for Patchwork and Quilting*, Book Number 5 (A Rowan Publication, 2003).

- *Anna Williams: Her Quilts and Their Influences*. (Katherine Watts, with Elizabeth Walker. American Quilter's Society, 1995).

- *Celtic Spirals and Other Designs* (Sheila Sturrock, Guild of Master Craftman Publications LTD, 2000). History and examples of Celtic designs.

- *Color Confidence for Quilters* (Jinny Beyer, The Quilt Digest Press, 1992).

- *Designing Tessellations: The Secrets of Interlocking Patterns* (Jinny Beyer, 1999). Presents ideas for designing tessellations.

- *Easy Does It Quilts* (Georgia Bonesteel, Oxmoor House, 1995).

- *Great Patchwork: Working With Squares and Triangles* (Meredith Corporation, 1995). Presents ideas for colorful gridded designs.

- *Intuitive Color and Design, Adventures in Art Quilting* (Jean Wells, C&T Publishing, 2009). Detailing a move toward the abstract.

- *Journey of an Art Quilter: Creative Strategies and Techniques*. Barbara Olson, Dragon Treads, 2004.

- *Make A Quilt In A Day: Log Cabin Patterns* (Eleanor Burns, Quilt In A Day, 2000). Countless design suggestions for log cabins.

- *M.C. Escher: 29 Master Prints* (Harry N. Abrams, Inc., 1971). A look at some amazing drawn tessellations.

- *Nancy Crow* (Breckling Press, 2006). A book about one quilter's journey into the abstract.

- *Oriental Carpets: Their Iconology and Iconography From Earliest Times to the 18th Century* (Taschen, 1998). History and examples of Oriental designs.

- *Rug Hooking* magazine, March/April/May 1993. Examples of traditional Nova Scotia inch mats.

- *The Quilts of Gee's Bend* (Tinwood Books, 2002). History and examples of African-American strip quilting.

- Various book on M. C. Escher, Victor Vasarely.